BRIGHTON

THE CENTURY IN PHOTOGRAPHS

VOLUME 1

CHRISTOPHER HORLOCK

DEDICATION

This, my first book on Brighton, is dedicated to my wonderful wife and family, Roz, Charlotte and George. The latter two (presently aged seven and four), don't really know what all the fuss has been about with all these funny old photographs, but one day, hopefully, they will . . .

First published in 2000 by S. B. Publications
c/o 19 Grove Road, Seaford
East Sussex BN25 1TP
01323 893498

ISBN 1 85770 198 4

Typeset by JEM Editorial
Printed by Adland Print Group Limited
Unit 11 Bellingham Trading Estate
Franthorne Way
London SE6 3BX
0181 695 6262

ACKNOWLEDGEMENTS

The photographs in this book are mainly from my own collection, but several postcard collectors and historian friends have allowed me free access to their collections and generously permitted the reproduction of certain views needed to make this book comprehensive.

So, in no special order, thanks are due to Robert Jeeves, worthy chairman of the Sussex Postcard Club and proprietor of Branch Two, the Postcard Saloon, in Queen's Road (where very nice enlarged copies of most of his collection are on sale), and Trevor Povey, the great Shoreham historian, who has given me many Brighton views over the years: I've lost track of what they were in many instances, but I know several here originate from him.

I must also thank Stephanie Green of Brighton Reference Library for allowing several pictures from the library's vast archives to appear. The *Evening Argus* gave permission for many of the more up-to-date pictures to be used, for which picture editor Richard Taylor and feature writer Paul Holden are to be thanked.

I'm also extremely grateful to Bob Elliston of Eastbourne, a friend now of many years, whose vast knowledge of Brighton's transport systems and the war years helped the caption research no end. Some of his photographs are featured here too.

Various other individuals and firms who have helped me with photographs, specific information or copyright clearance are Alan Hayes, the well-known local fisherman; Trevor Cox, paddle steamer expert; Stephen Horlock, for pictures of the

Athina B; David Store of Ordnance Survey, for permission to reproduce maps; Tony McKendrick Warden, postcard dealer, for several pictures; Terry Charman of the Imperial War Museum, London, for information about World War One; Richard Lindfield for Brighton and Hove Albion facts and figures; John Davey, Estates Manager of Brighton Marina, for information about redevelopment; Jacqueline Pollard for allowing part of a taped interview to be reproduced, plus information on Cox's factory.

Much of the necessary photographic work for the book was carried out by Tom Reeves of Lewes; if you enjoy all the small details to be found in the early photographs, it's mostly because of the trouble he's taken. I must also thank various work colleagues, particularly Martin Oborne, for showing me all the tricks needed for getting the text onto floppy disk.

Finally, I have to record the debt I owe to the late James Gray (1904-1998), whose phenomenal knowledge of the town was freely passed on to me during frequent visits to his home in Shirley Avenue, Hove, over nearly a twenty year period. He gave me many of his spare photographs, some of which appear here for the first time in print. His own collection, some thirty-nine massive volumes, is now the property of the Regency Society of Brighton and Hove and is the most important set of annotated Brighton and Hove photographs the town possesses.

SOURCES AND REFERENCES

There's no doubt that local newspapers were the best source material when compiling the captions for this book. Back numbers of the *Evening Argus*, the *Sussex Daily News, Brighton and Hove Gazette* and *Brighton and Hove Herald*, were all consulted (many times!) to verify dates, events, statistics etc. The other best source was the individuals named in the acknowledgements, experts in specific areas, all of whom generously took time to respond by letter or phone to requests for obscure information.

A large number of lecture notes used by James Gray were passed on to me, which were invaluable for basic dates, facts and figures. The main books consulted were period guidebooks (principally those published by Ward Lock); *Life In Brighton*, by Clifford Musgrave (John Halliwell Publications, 1970); *Brighton's Music Halls*, by David Adland (Baron Birch, 1994); *Dr Brighton's Patients,* by Joyce Collins (Brighton Books Publishing, 1997); *Brighton Old And New,* by Antony Dale and James Gray (E P Publishing, 1976); *Brighton Between The Wars*, by James Gray (Batsford, 1976); *Brighton Encyclopaedia*, by Tim Carder (East Sussex County Libraries, 1990).

SPECIAL NOTE

Distances and measurements are given in old imperial units. I'm sure anyone who really needs the metric equivalents will be able to work them out. Amounts of money are also given in old pounds, shillings and pence. Basically, before metrication in 1971, there were twenty shillings in a pound and twelve pennies to a shilling. So ten shillings (written as 10/-) would be 50p today, three shillings (written 3/-) would be 15p and so on. Two pounds and two shillings, written as £2/2/-, would be £2.10 today. There were 240 pence in a pound, so 120 pence made 10/-. **CH**

CONTENTS

One hundred years ago stylish Meeting House Lane was neglected, poorly lit, almost run down. See page 33.

Introduction – Cockles and Culture,
Treasure and Trash 5

The early 1900s 8

World War I 49

The 1920s 54

The 1930s 74

World War II 86

The 1940s and 1950s 92

The 1960s 101

The 1970s and 1980s 117

The 1990s 135

About the Author 144

COCKLES AND CULTURE, TREASURE AND TRASH

No seaside town has the richness of past history and present day amenity that Brighton can boast. The Pavilion and its royal associations, the town's extraordinary architectural heritage, the famous seafront, piers and Lanes area, its theatre and club scene, these are just some of the elements that fuse to create a town that is cultural but raffish, a place for simple fun or serious instruction, the town Sir John Betjeman called 'a toyshop for London,' a resort unique, unrivalled and almost intoxicating in its freshness and day to day 'frisson'.

This heady mix of cockles and culture has pervaded since the 1750s, when Lewes physician, Dr Richard Russell, advised those suffering from various glandular disorders to find relief through sea bathing – the so-called 'salt-water cure'. The town soon had an influx of wealthy visitors keen to try the idea and almost immediately provided the first theatre, ballrooms, bath buildings and racecourse, which would now be termed 'resort facilities', and can be seen as early elements of the pleasure town Brighton would become.

The visits (from 1783) and later residency of George, Prince of Wales, later George IV, gave enormous impetus to the development of the town during the early 1800s, and the coming of the railway in 1841 saw the mushrooming of hotels and amenities on a quite unprecedented scale.

In short, Brighton has always responded to the need of providing diversion and novelty. This has been equally true of the twentieth century, which has seen mixed fortunes for the town and certainly did not start well. Brighton's huge Victorian popularity had led to a lethargic decline and the town coasted along during the early 1900s, doing very little to sort out mounting overcrowding, traffic build up or stagnating facilities. This complacency, as the book shows, was halted and completely turned round in the 1920s, and the period between the wars can be rightly seen as

At the turn of the century, visitors stream off the train from London for a day beside the sea.

Brighton's glory days, for both residents and visitors, with cheap public transport (the trams), clean sea to bathe in, flourishing theatres and cinemas (fourteen cinemas in the late 1930s), trains that ran on time, an industrial heart to the town, slum clearance and housing needs being addressed, road widening, new buildings going up – even the sun shone!

In the post-war period Brighton's priorities shifted from the holiday trade to conference facilities. Industry slipped away or died out, much housing in the central area was lost and offices sprang up everywhere, with no-one forseeing the enormous parking problems places like the American Express complex in Edward Street would bring. Some of the worst buildings the town possesses went up in this period, when high-rise was seemingly the architectural answer to everything.

Quite where all this leaves Brighton in 2000 is hard to judge. The recent amalgamation with Hove should have made the city of Brighton and Hove a reality, and this must be something that will happen very soon. But Brighton seems unsure about its identity or what it stands for as the century turns. A cultural centre? A tripper town? One enormous conference facility? Except at the Pavilion, its amazing history is inexplicably neglected, the quite extraordinary range of Victorian churches it possesses go uncelebrated and the town's architecture has developed into an alarming mix of treasure and trash. There is still a huge question mark over the West Pier, closed for thirty years; the old chestnuts of traffic congestion and car parking generally drift on and the town seems about to seize up totally. Also a certain tackiness has descended that is easy to sense but hard to define. Brighton appears to have tried hard to be even extra trendy as the century closes, with a spate of theme pubs opening and silly names being given to older ones, losing historic links with the areas they stand in.

On the other hand, much that is positive has been achieved. The seafront looks better than it has for years, the town has a fine and friendly fishing museum, the Palace Pier has been revitalised and the Marina at last stands more like it was originally meant to, with a large number of attractions and amenities for non-sailing visitors. The Brighton Festival continues to flourish, venues for fringe theatre have been established and the Dome complex is being renovated and modernised. Some housing is creeping back into the town centre and the new Churchill Square shopping complex, whatever may be thought of its design, has been a success. A new library has been promised for early in the next century and millions have recently been spent on renovating the station.

If you quickly flick through this book, the whole century passes, somewhat disturbingly, in a matter of seconds. The changes to the fabric and topography of the town naturally form the main interest, but what of the people in the pictures? How have they been affected? People don't change, it is said, but I think they do and I am sure they have.

In the early 1900s, people seemed far more religious, had to work harder for longer hours, were generous of spirit, but were insular, much less credulous, quite narrow-minded and often stubborn and set in their ways. They did not travel far, accepted their lot in life and had few ambitions. The class system was rigidly set and people knew their place within it. The streets they lived in were their world, their communities; today streets are just places to park cars.

People aren't like that now. In post-war times, church-going habits have severely declined, people still have to work hard, but loyalty to a firm or business is completely a thing of the past. People are far more open-minded and easy going, but more ambitious, many extremely materialistic, wanting possessions instantly – particularly 'designer' goods – that their parents and grandparents saved months or even years for.

People are probably no more aggressive now than then, but there seems more assertiveness about, more day-to-day intolerance of which 'road rage' and 'neighbours from hell', were just two 1990s manifestations.

Something of the values of each generation dies out with them of course, but attitudes and outlook are also shaped by influences beyond individual control. The way we have to communicate, do our shopping, bank our money, engage services, travel around and so on have been imposed by businesses or firms to suit their ends, not ours. Despite all that is said about service, the customer no longer comes first at all. Not even a good second.

So look too at the people in the pages of this book. How they have changed and been changed by the circumstances of twentieth century living is just as significant and fascinating as the physical changes to the streets they are in or the buildings that surround them.

What are our values now compared to theirs? What really

New Year's Eve, 1998, when 10,000 packed into Old Steine to welcome the penultimate year of the century

is our outlook on life as the century turns? In 2000, are we any happier or more fulfilled than they were then? Or with our credit cards and computers, and every comfort and amenity around us, do we just pretend we are?

Christopher Horlock, February 2000

ARRIVAL OF VISITORS
As the railway station was the gateway into Brighton for the majority of visitors this century, it seems the logical place to start this look at Brighton over the last 100 years.

This view of about 1905 shows the place jam-packed with visitors about to stream into the town, down Queen's Road and West Street, to the seafront area, where the pleasures of the piers and beaches awaited them. The huge canopy above the platforms, dating from 1882-83, would have seemed very impressive for a provincial station.

Brighton's popularity as a resort would peak over the next three decades, then decline after World War Two when cheap trips abroad became more common and the British seaside holiday waned in popularity.

BRIGHTON STATION, THE LOCOMOTIVE SHEDS

To the north of the station area, beyond the platforms, were the locomotive running sheds, this view dating from October 1908. Over 40 engines stand 'coaled-up', ready to take carriages. The photograph was taken on a Sunday, so these engines would have brought weekend trippers to the town; often over a hundred trains would be laid on at weekends to meet demand. It was the railway reaching Brighton in 1841 that opened up the town to the tripper and holidaymaker, causing huge impetus to the development of the town's amenities, particularly in the 1860s and 1870s.

WEST STREET

A turn of the century view, showing trippers strolling down narrow West Street to reach the sea. They can walk anywhere they like, traffic is so minimal.

The Clock Tower at the top of the street, was built in 1888 to commemorate the Golden Jubilee of Queen Victoria the previous year. It is seen in the summer of

1902, when it was illuminated to celebrate the coronation of Edward VII. Turkish Baths, of 1868, are on the left of the main picture, where the huge lantern hangs. These would be converted into the Academy Cinema in 1911.

West Street would be widened between 1925 and 1963 and all the buildings to the right, except St Paul's Church, would come down for this. New buildings, such as the SS Brighton swimming pool and an Odeon cinema, would subsequently replace them, set back on the new building line.

KING'S ROAD

So to the seafront, where visitors could walk along the prom, sit in the sun or visit one of the piers. The huge lamp-posts which still stand on Brighton seafront – but now with different tops – date from 1893, when King's Road was first lit by electricity.

Muttons, below, was a famous hotel and restaurant at 81-84 King's Road. It was established in 1820 by William Sexton Mutton, although the extended premises in the photograph date from the 1840s. It featured in the 1866 book *Mattins And Muttons* by Cuthbert Bede. Muttons closed in 1929 and the buildings were eventually cleared, after various ownerships, for the Top Rank development the 1960s.

Notice Thomas Cook's travel agency on the right. In the early 1900s, a week in Paris would have cost £4/14/6, eleven days in Germany, by rail, £5/5/0, and two weeks in Switzerland, £7/7/0.

THE GRAND HOTEL

Only very rich visitors would be able to afford a stay at one of the town's seafront hotels, such as the Grand, seen here about 1912. Notice it advertises a garage – the wealthy were arriving at Brighton in their cars now. The Grand is easily the most delightful and stylish of all Brighton's top hotels, standing today largely rebuilt and enlarged following the terrorist bombing outrage of October 1984. It opened in July 1864 and was the first hotel in the town to have lifts. The wine list ran to 200 varieties.

Most holidaymakers of the early 1900s would probably stay at a

boarding house or rent an apartment, such as in German Place, above, running from Marine Parade to St James's Street.

A stay at a typical boarding house during the early 1900s would cost about 3/- a night. An average room in the Grand Hotel would have been in the region of 10/-.

THE LOWER PROMENADE

The crowds seen in the previous views have dispersed and many would be on the beaches or piers. On the lower prom, seen in this view about 1908, every kind of refreshment was available for the hungry visitor. Teas and lunches are for sale on the left (a full lunch would have cost about 1/-), the Fortune Of War pub is between the two buildings with awnings and several beach stalls have

BRIGHTON. Lower Esplanade. PPCo?

shellfish for sale. The arches and railings on this part of Brighton seafront date from the widening of King's Road in 1885-86. The date 1886 can be found on most of the end posts of each section of railings, with a helmet above, both in heavy relief. Then it was thought that the town took its old Brighthelmstone name from an ancient chief who wore a 'bright helm'. This idea has now been outmoded and today, *Beorthelm's Tun*, meaning Beorthelm's farm is the usual derivation, but even this isn't certain. The name of Brighton was officially taken in 1810.

PUNCH AND JUDY SHOW

All manner of itinerant entertainment animated Brighton's lower promenade and beach area in the first half of the century – buskers and musicians of all kinds, strongmen, acrobats, jugglers, fire-eaters, ventriloquists, even orators who acted out scenes from famous plays, could all be found dotted along the seafront, particularly either side of the West Pier. One of the more unusual acts was Black Charlie, a giant,

grinning negro, who drew gasps of disbelief from onlookers as he threw sticks up to enormous heights and caught them again. He claimed that he could throw a stick from the entrance of the West Pier clear over the top of the Hotel Metropole, a quite staggering distance.

In the photograph here, a traditional Punch and Judy show takes place, about 1902, opposite the Queen's Hotel. If the people up at the rail are included, then more adults than children are watching. Punch and Judy showmen often had a real Toby dog with them, to draw a crowd, seen behind the booth, bottom left.

BEACH ENTERTAINMENT

A huge crowd gathers to watch the Highwaymen concert party's performance on a makeshift stage near the West Pier. The group was founded in 1905 by Frank Gomm (his stage name was Jack Sheppard), who continued running concert party groups on the seafront right up to World War Two. In the line-up, opposite, he stands on the extreme left. He died in 1968, aged ninety-four, at his home in Rugby Place.

The stage here was officially known as the Cannon Place Entertainment Stand. It survived until early 1929 when it was removed due to no-one booking it for the forthcoming season.

THE FISHMARKET

For centuries Brighton's fishermen had sold their catches straight from the beach. During the 1840s, room was made for them in the town's general market – in Market Street – but the fishermen wanted premises of their own, close to the beach, where they had always operated.

The first purpose-built fishmarket opened in December 1867 from brick arches specially built on the lower promenade. When King's Road was widened, nearly twenty years later, a number of new, red brick arches were given over to the fishermen to house their market. Ramps running from King's Road to the lower promenade were installed (still there) to give easy access for horse and cart traffic.

Catches being sold outside on the market hard inadvertently became another tourist attraction, as seen here about 1905.

The market was the source of fresh fish for many of the seafront hotels, restaurants and boarding houses. At this time twenty herring cost 1/-. Large quantities were sold by Dutch auction – that is, starting with the highest bid and working downwards.

THE WEST PIER

Everyone, whatever class or background, rich or poor, old and young alike, went on the piers when visiting Brighton.

The West Pier, designed by Eusebius Birch, was built between 1863 and 1866 at a cost of £35,000. It opened in October 1866, and is rightly seen as the finest example of pier design and engineering in the country.

At first, it was just a promenade pier, devoid of most of the buildings and the attractions seen here. These were added from 1890 onwards and included the large concert pavilion and extensive landing stages for paddle steamer excursions. The pavilion was converted into a theatre in 1903. This had seating for 1,076 people and was used for concerts, variety shows,

musicals and plays. A knockabout show called *Casey's Court*, featured young Charlie Chaplin and Stan Laurel at the start of their careers. Many other well-known performers appeared here over the years including Ellen Terry, Edith Evans, Rex Harrison, Ralph Richardson, Ronald Colman, Cicely Courtenage, Robert Morley and James Whale, who would later find fame as a Hollywood director, responsible for the Frankenstein films, featuring Boris Karloff.

The pier was closed during World War Two, but the theatre never reopened and was converted into an amusement arcade.

ON THE WEST PIER

A typical view of the pier-head, about 1905. This was a place for fashionable people to gather, promenade, and involve themselves in what we would call 'people-watching' today.

Whatever else may be of interest here, there is always enormous poignancy in any photograph taken just before World War One, where young men are seen, like the one under the fancy sunshade. In a few years' time he will almost certainly experience all the ghastly horrors of trench warfare with its shelling, mud-filled dugouts and gas poisoning, which couldn't be further removed from the gaiety and carelessness of the scene here; the day he spent strolling with his sweetheart, in the sun, on the pier at Brighton.

THE PALACE PIER

The Palace Pier – its longer original name of The Brighton Marine Palace And Pier was soon dropped for all but official purposes – was a brand new attraction for the town as the century turned. It had opened in May 1899, after taking more than seven years to build. There was a second opening in April 1901, when the theatre – called the Marine Palace – was completed.

The view above, taken from the Royal Albion Hotel, shows the pier in about 1903. As well as the theatre, its attractions were the simple pleasures of band concerts, sitting in a kiosk to chat and enjoy the sea air, playing the slot machines, or taking a paddle steamer excursion to other resorts such as Eastbourne or Hastings, or westwards to the Isle of Wight.

There was a bathing station under the pier-head where swimmers could enjoy a bathe in deep water, away from the crowds and noise of the beach.

The designer of the pier was Richard St George More, and the initial cost was £137,000.

THE PALACE PIER THEATRE

A close-up of the pier theatre, plus a view of the 1,500-seat interior, both dating from about 1903. The design of the building, like the rest of the pier, was clearly influenced by the look of the Royal Pavilion; even the inside looked oriental, very different from the West Pier's traditional auditorium. A windbreak was installed down the centre of the pier in 1906 to make the journey to the theatre more comfortable, The theatre itself was considerably altered inside and out in 1910-11, when huge investment was made to add to the attractions and amenities, including a winter garden, which later became the Palace of Fun. Among those who began their careers with the Palace Pier repertory company were Hermione Gingold, Julie Christie and Judy Cornwell.

BRIGHTON 190

OLD CHAIN PIER

S. Hellier, 48 Kings Road, Brighton — 183

POSTCARD OF THE CHAIN PIER

As the century began, visitors could buy this postcard view of a Brighton pier that didn't exist! The town's famous Chain Pier was swept away by a storm in December 1896; in its day it was considered one of the great sights of southern Britain. It opened in November 1823 and stood opposite New Steine, going out from the cliff where the shops on Maderia Drive were later built. It was erected on wooden piles with four sets of iron towers spaced along the length of the pier, linked together with chain-link cables fixed to massive steel plates buried fifty feet into the cliff. Essentially the pier was a landing stage for steam packet ships taking goods and passengers to and from the continent. The pier's slow demise began when the railway reached Newhaven Harbour in December 1847, completely diverting traffic away from Brighton.

VOLK'S ELECTRIC RAILWAY

Volk's Electric Railway, the first in Britain, was a great novelty for visitors to the town; it still runs along the seafront, but not over the sea as once it used to.

The invention of Magnus Volk – who lived in Dyke Road near the Seven Dials – the railway began running in August 1883, from the Aquarium to the Chain Pier. Instant popularity with trippers led to its extension to Paston Place the following year, and to Black Rock (its destination today) in 1901.

Initially the seaside railway was unpopular with cabmen and fisherman running boat trips, who thought it would take their trade away.

Magnus Volk, the son of a German clockmaker, was a child prodigy who enjoyed experimenting with electrical gadgets from an early age. As a young man he

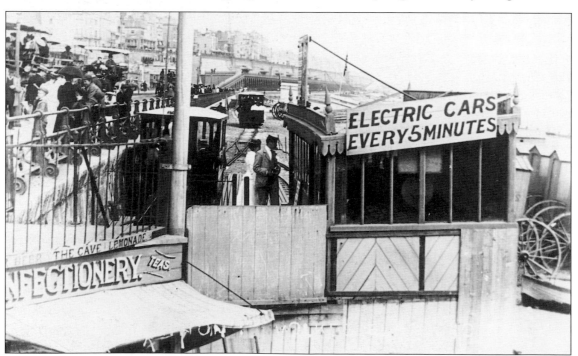

equipped his house with the first domestic electric lights in the town and he also had his own telephone system. By 1883, when his railway opened, he had illuminated the Royal Pavilion with electricity.

The small sea wall, behind the line (seen through the railings, left), had been built in 1870 with blocks from the first Blackfriars Bridge in London; this had been demolished in 1863.

In 1999, the *Guinness Book of Records* announced the line would be listed as the oldest surviving electric railway in the world.

THE ELECTRIC SEASHORE TRAMROAD

This extraordinary vehicle, resembling a tramcar on legs, could be found on Brighton's seafront between 1896 and 1901, taking visitors to Rottingdean and back via a seabed track-way some three miles in length.

At high tide the ride was at its most exhilarating, although the speed was comparatively slow at some six miles an hour. Passengers embarked from a specially built pier adjoining the Banjo Groyne; the journey was 1/- return and, depending on the sea conditions, took about thirty-five minutes each way.

The venture was another project of the Brighton inventor and engineer, Magnus Volk. Originally known as the Brighton And Rottingdean Electric Seashore Tramroad, it was soon nicknamed Daddy Longlegs; because of its spider-like appearance.

The originality of the tramroad attracted a great deal of interest; even the *New York Herald* got to hear of it and commented: 'Mechanically, and as a seashore novelty, beats anything yet done by us inventive Yankees'.

It closed after only four years when Brighton Corporation decided to extend the groynes on this section of the beach. To continue, Volk would have had to divert his line further out to sea, which would have been impractical.

ON THE BEACH

From the technological wonder seen on the previous page, to the most basic of all Brighton's seafront pleasures – a paddle! Is this all one family posing for the camera near the West Pier, about 1912? Several people resemble each other, so it's possible. The man with the cigarette doesn't seem too happy, but the others appear to be enjoying their paddle. The boys in the centre show signs of rickets (knock-knees) caused by vitamin deficiencies in their diet, which was common at this time.

As with any old photograph of people, it's fascinating to look at the rows of faces and wonder what these people were like and what became of them. Again, the poignancy of some of the men having to serve in World War One won't go away. There is just a chance that at this turn of the millennium, one or two of the very young children here are still alive. What a century of change they will have seen!

THE ALHAMBRA THEATRE

Just east of the Grand Hotel, the Alhambra was the ideal place for a night at the music hall. This view shows the  King's Road entrance about 1905; the main façade and entrance was round the corner, to the left, in Russell Street. Originally the theatre was to have been named the Eden, but it opened as the Alhambra Opera House and Music Hall in October 1888.

Most of the late Victorian and Edwardian variety stars appeared at the Alhambra, including Marie Lloyd (above), Florrie Ford, Dan Leno, George Robey (below), Sandow the Strongman, singer Charles Chaplin (father of Charlie), magician Chung Ling Soo and Mark Sheridan, who is remembered for the song *Oh, I Do Like To Be Beside The Seaside*. With them came supporting acts – acrobats, jugglers, wire walkers, trick cyclists, contortionists, tank swimmers, illusionists, mimics, ventriloquists, mesmerists, strong men and women, trapeze artistes, giants, dwarfs, boxers and animal acts of every kind. Of these lesser stars, Mlle Diane de Fortenoy caused a stir several times by posing naked in a series of tableaux. Nude acts were not uncommon, being seen as artistic celebrations of the female form.

THE INTERIOR OF THE ALHAMBRA

The breathtaking interior of the 2,000-seat Alhambra, photographed about 1910, is all the more astonishing considering its converted shop front entrance from the seafront, seen on the previous page.

On the opening night, in October 1888, the great American tightrope walker, Charles Fontaine, made his entrance sliding down a wire stretched from the upper balcony to the stage. He later went back up, on stilts!

The designer of the theatre was Frank Matcham who was also responsible for the Brighton Hippodrome as well as the London Coliseum and the London Palladium. Between 1879 and 1912, he designed some 150 theatres, virtually a quarter of all those built during the period. In 1903, he supervised alterations to the Devonshire Park Theatre, Eastbourne.

From 1892, a new novelty was introduced at the Alhambra, known as the 'Edisonograph'. Some of the first moving pictures to be seen in Brighton were included as part of the show. In their later form, of course, these would be the death of the music hall and variety.

The Alhambra Theatre was converted into the Grand Cinema De Luxe in April 1912, and survived, as a cinema, with several changes of name and two new façades, until May 1956.

QUEEN'S ELECTRIC THEATRE

There's no doubt that as the century turned, 'animated pictures' were the entertainment novelty everyone wanted to see. Brighton was quick to respond to this trend with most theatres, including those on the piers, showing films as a finale to their variety bills.

At the same time, in West Street, film shows were taking place in a large concert hall; a little later, about 1910, even the Salvation Army Congress Hall in Union Place was used for showing films. A number of small purpose-built cinemas also opened up in the town. The first of these seems to have been on the seafront opposite the West Pier, called Pandora's Gallery. This operated from March 1896. The cinema shown here, in 1911, is the Queen's Electric Theatre, on the northern side of Western Road, near the corner of Montpelier Road (off to the left). Originally a smaller building, housing extremely basic equipment, it opened in January 1909 and was extended in 1910.

Programmes consisted of comedy shorts, over-the-top dramas and Pathe's Animated Gazette. Surprisingly, operas were shown, with words and music supplied by a device known as the 'Animatophone'.

A cinema continued on the site until 1979.

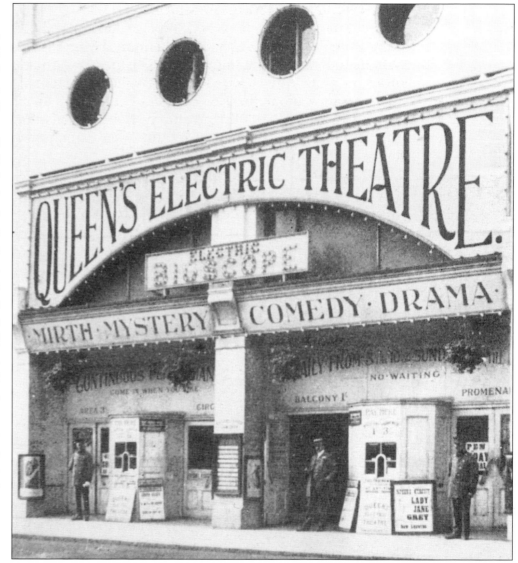

THE GEM CINEMA

Another early cinema, opening in 1910, was the Gem, at 36a London Road, seen here about 1912. It stood on the western side, roughly half way between Ann Street and York Hill.

A converted shop, it accommodated about sixty customers on plain wooden benches.

One film known to have been shown was the world heavyweight boxing match between Jack Johnson and Jim Jefferies, fought in Reno, Nevada, in July 1910. In the winter of 1912, the popular Highwaymen concert party (page 15), gave a series of indoor concerts here.

Competition from the purpose-built Duke of York Cinema at Preston Circus, which had also opened in 1910, forced the Gem to close in 1915.

BRIGHTON AND HOVE ALBION FOOTBALL GROUND

Sporting entertainment as the century began was much more limited than it is today, but here is Brighton and Hove Albion's football ground, about 1910. It's quite clear how most fans reached the game!

Brighton's first fully professional team, founded in 1898, had been Brighton United, whose players had to use the cricket ground at Hove to play on. This team was succeeded by Brighton and Hove Rangers then, in 1902, Brighton and Hove Albion was founded. The team's ground, originally a field belonging to Goldstone Farm, had opened in September 1902, initially for Hove Football Club. The Albion's first match there was in February the following year.

Early managers were John Jackson from 1900, Frank Scott-Walford from 1905 and John Robson from 1908.

EAST STREET

As now, visitors to Brighton would have liked to look round the shops, to browse and see what was new. East Street, in the Old Town area, almost certainly Brighton's oldest street, was a popular place for this. The photograph, looking north, was taken just up from the seafront end of the street, about 1908 and, because the scale and proportion of the street has been retained, the view is still recognisable. A Brighton guidebook of 1907, titled *Beautiful, Breezy Brighton*, stated: 'The shops of Brighton are worthy of careful study; one of their leading characteristics is that they are altogether destitute of a provincial aspect: you might fancy yourself in Regent Street, or Piccadilly, or in Bond Street, for here you can obtain the millinery, the hosiery, the gloves, the hats, the jewellery, the fans, the lingerie, which you can procure in London.' This was just the sort of comparison that gave Brighton the nickname of 'London By The Sea'.

WEST STREET

West Street, probably the second oldest street in Brighton, was seen on page 10, but this is the eastern side, which would survive large-scale redevelopment, although a fair number of individual buildings have been altered or demolished. One of these was the large concert hall, in the centre, dating from 1867. This building had a long but chequered history, seeing many different uses over

GRAND CONCERT HALL
West Street, Brighton.
Every Day at 3 and 8.
Continued Success
of the Great
AMERICAN BIOGARPH
Direct from the
PALACE THEATRE, LONDON.
Augmented by a
High-Class Concert Party.
Great Enthusiasm over the
GRAND NEW PICTURES.
Last Week, positively closing SATURDAY, JANUARY 12th.
Matinees 4s., 3s., 2s., 1s. Evenings 3s., 2s , 1s.
Children under 12 half-price
Plan of Room and Tickets at Messrs. Lyon and Hall's, Warwick Mansions, Brighton, and 22 Church-road, Hove.

the years. In the 1870s the explorer Sir Henry Morton Stanley ('Dr Livingstone, I presume?') lectured here, as did the surgeon Frederick Treves, who is remembered for his association with John Merrick, the 'Elephant Man', and for removing Edward VII's appendix prior to his coronation in 1902.

The concert hall building became a skating rink in 1877, was wrecked by a gas explosion and fire in 1882, reopened ten years later as another skating rink, was converted to a cinema (the advertisement, left, dates from January 1901), then in 1911 became a restaurant. In 1918 it was the Coliseum Picture Theatre and in 1919 it became a dance hall, taking the legendary name Sherrys, which was immortalised in Graham Green's book *Brighton Rock*.

NORTH STREET

The third of the town's oldest streets is seen in this view, about 1910, looking east to Castle Square and Old Steine. The covered walkway, on the left, known as the Royal Colonnade, ran from outside 157 North Street, round the corner into New Road and along to the Theatre Royal, where a small section still stands today. Most of it was removed in the 1920s.

On the other side of the road, on the extreme right, is the Clarence Hotel, originally the New Inn of 1785, which is still there today, but as Clarence House, occupied by the Portman Building Society. The tower of the Chapel Royal can also be seen, dating from 1882. The large building in the centre, in almost baroque style, was very new at the time of this photograph, dating from 1904. Today it houses the Halifax Building Society.

The London and Midland bank, in the small picture, seen about 1900, occupied a site at the junction of Ship Street (left) and North Street. In 1903 the bank moved to 151-153 North Street, later becoming just the Midland Bank.

MEETING HOUSE LANE

Today, the heart of the Old Town area, known as The Lanes, is a principal tourist attraction, with its narrow street pattern, open-air restaurants and wine bars, antiques, art and fashion shops.

Yet in the early 1900s, the area was neglected, poorly lit, almost run down, as this photograph shows. There were a large number of 'object d'art' shops, plus booksellers, a few pubs, a barber shop or two, shoe repair premises, and so on. No attempt was made to make the place attractive to visitors until the 1930s, when there were proposals to rebuild most of the area. Nothing happened, mainly due to World War Two, but eventually, in 1966, Brighton Square was created, revitalising the whole area.

Meeting House Lane, where the photograph was taken, once led to a very ancient non-conformist chapel in Union Street, which a plaque on the present building – the Font and Firkin pub – states stood as long ago as 1688, with rebuilding taking place in 1810.

THE HIPPODROME

Another venue for an evening's show was the Hippodrome in Middle Street, seen here about 1900. This building began as an ice-rink, opening early in 1897, run by brothers Ellis and Humphrey Brammall. Wanting a more profitable venture, they had Frank Matcham, the celebrated theatre designer, convert the rink into a circus theatre – a ring plus a proscenium stage – enabling circus acts to alternate with variety turns. This opened in August 1901, as the Hippodrome Theatre of Varieties. Like the ice-rink, it was not a particularly successful undertaking and the Brammall brothers sold up. New managers, Barrasford and Smith took over, promptly removed the ring, put stalls seating in its place and opened their new variety theatre in December 1902. For more than sixty years, it never looked back.

Middle Street School, Brighton's oldest, can be seen in the distance, on the extreme left of the picture on page 34. This was founded in 1805, the year of the Battle of Trafalgar.

The picture below was taken inside the wonderfully ornate Hippodrome, about 1905, showing the stage, boxes and stalls. During its sixty-three-year history, the theatre saw the transition from music hall through to full-blown, twice-nightly variety, from opera to the town's first pop concerts. It also presented plays, ballets, revues, musicals, Gilbert and Sullivan operettas and all the big dance bands of the day. Anyone and everyone appeared at the 'Hippo'. Early stars included Sarah Bernhardt, Marie Lloyd, Vesta Tilley (pictured right) who is said to haunt the theatre, Little Titch, Harry Lauder, escapologist Harry Houdini (below), and illusionist The Great Lafayette.

In the inter-war years came such names as Gracie Fields, the Crazy Gang, Vivien Leigh, Stanley Holloway, Raymond Massey, Jessie Matthews, Gladys Cooper, plus the dance bands of Henry Hall, Joe Loss, Harry Roy and Billy Cotton.

35

THE BLACK LION BREWERY

In Black Lion Street, leading to the sea (left in this view), visitors could find a real piece of old Brighton still standing – the Black Lion Brewery. It is seen here, up for sale, in 1912, eleven years after brewing had ceased. This was the ancient brewery from which the street took its name. At the time of this photograph, it was the oldest brewery building in the world. The low cobbled portion, which once had three dormer windows, was still thought to be in its original Tudor form, dating back to the 1540s. Hops would have been grown very close to the brewery, in a part

of the Lanes that was then known as the Hempshares.

The building was once said to be owned by Protestant martyr Deryck Carver, who was burnt at the stake in Lewes in 1555 during the Marian persecutions.

The cobbled section was demolished in about 1930; a similarly proportioned building, but with a higher roof, took its place. The brewery itself survived until 1968, with office and showrooms built on the site of the southern section in 1975. All that remains today is a replica of the granary loft, operating as a pub, and some of the old cellars.

ST JAMES'S STREET

A really lively, bustling view of St James's Street, looking east, about 1910. On the right, a shopkeeper seems to have brought his whole family out to pose for the camera – even the baby!

This was the principle shopping area for eastern Brighton, where, over the years, many well-known firms had premises including Boots the Chemist (still there in 2000), Woolworths, Sainsburys, Clark's shoes, Liptons the grocers and Galliers, electrical engineers.

The street has largely survived road widening and still keeps something of its past scale and character. In 1999 several ideas were put forward to modernise the street, including making the western (Old Steine) end a pedestrian precinct.

St James's Street dates from about 1785. A map of 1799 shows the lower part of the street called Craven Buildings, then from Charles Street, the name changes to Prospect Row. The present name, adopted about 1803, is said to come from the royal residence, St James's Palace, in London.

EDWARD STREET

This view, looking east from Grand Parade, was taken about 1900. The street is extremely narrow compared with how it stands today, the result of redevelopment over a period of fifty years, starting in the 1920s with the corner building on the left. All the clearance work took place on this side, so most of what stands on the southern side still exists, including the cobble-fronted building (extreme right) dating from about 1790.

Edward Street developed from the very early 1800s, and was supposedly named after Queen Victoria's father. It was considered a tough, almost 'no go' area from the late 1800s through to the 1930s, and it's said that policemen always patrolled in pairs.

In 1890 there were twenty-six pubs and beer shops in the quarter-mile length of the street – roughly one every seventeen paces!

Slightly earlier, in streets on the sites of White Street and Blaker Street, the foulest slums in the whole town – later cleared in the 1890s – could be found, along with the town's 'red-light' district.

LONDON ROAD

London Road is seen here in 1904, following widening on the western (right) side to allow for the tram system laid out in the previous year. A tram can be seen beyond the carriage, and on the left is Baker Street.

London Road was originally named Queen's Road. Once just a narrow track connecting Brighton with the village of Preston, by 1845 it was built up from York Place to Preston Circus, on both sides, mostly by private houses; many of these houses has front gardens.

As late as 1892, of seventy-three buildings on the western side of London Road, half were shops, but half still houses. The coming of the trams gave added impetus to commercial development and by the early 1900s, virtually all the houses had been converted to shops, with living accommodation above.

LEWES ROAD

A view of Lewes Road at the junction with Elm Grove (to the right) dating from about 1903. The view looks northwards and the outline of St Martin's Church, completed in 1875, can be made out in the distance. It is the largest church – in terms of floor area – in the town. In among the shops in the centre, at 6 Lewes Road, was a postal and telegraphic office run by G F Bunney. A century later, a post office can still be found at the same location. The tram in the distance (right) is on a route between Natal Road and the Aquarium. The Race Hill Inn, centre, still stands, although now much altered and extended. The development of Lewes Road had started in 1795 with the building of cavalry barracks. These became Preston Barracks which have only recently been demolished. Until May 1999, the Territorial Army still occupied part of the site.

WESTERN ROAD

Several previous views of Brighton's main streets have still been recognisable, but with this one, nothing gives a clue that it's of the eastern end of Western Road, where today, Churchill Square stands off to the left and shops leading up to the Imperial Arcade entrance are on the right. The turning down to Upper Russell Street, a tiny part of which still exists, can be seen bottom left.

The road is now at least three times the width seen here. Buildings are decked out with flags and bunting for the coronation of Edward VII in the summer of 1902. The horse bus is probably a number 6, on its way to Portslade Station via Western Road and New Church Road. Western Road was originally a track-way running from North Street to the church at Hove, development beginning in the early 1800s.

CORONATION OF EDWARD VII

A fascinating story linking Edward VII and a Brighton fortune teller just has to be told at this point.

Gipsy Lee, who told visitors their fortunes from her caravan at Devil's Dyke, announced that Edward's coronation would not take place. This startled everyone as all the arrangements had been made and the date fixed for July 9, 1902.

Why wouldn't the King be crowned? Was a terrible disaster about to strike? Only the fortune teller wasn't surprised when news came that the coronation was postponed – the King had developed acute appendicitis! It was August 9 before he was eventually crowned. Gipsy Lee's fame was assured of course; no doubt the queues outside her caravan were especially long that season.

Gipsy Lee lived in Melbourne Street, taking a carriage to the Dyke each day, where she worked for nearly forty years. In 1904, she was fined for trading illegally. She then ran refreshment rooms for a while, but eventually she languished at an asylum in Haywards Heath, where she died in 1911.

HORSE BUSES

In 1900, horse buses were the main public transport in Brighton. This one was photographed about 1905, somewhere along the Preston Road, on the outskirts of the town. Its route was very straightforward, running between Preston village and Castle Square, via Preston Park.

Notice the huge rear wheel with its brake, the driver and people on the top deck, all exposed to the elements, also the bowler-hatted conductor with his change bag.

By 1905 however, in central Brighton, two new kinds of transport had begun operating – trams and motor buses – which would bring a complete end to horse buses by December 1916.

Trams ran along London Road, but not to Preston; the first motor bus to the village ran in December 1906.

KEMP TOWN AND LEWES ROAD STATIONS

Another way of travelling around Brighton in the early 1900s was by train. Preston Park station, on the main London line, had opened in November 1869; London Road, on the Lewes line, in October 1877. Before these though, in 1866, a new, separate line was built, branching off the Lewes Line, then curving south to reach Kemp Town. This was the mile and a quarter Kemp Town line, which opened in August 1869. It was a costly and complex route to build, requiring a viaduct spanning Lewes Road, a bridge over Hartington Road, then a tunnel, some 1,000 yards long, under Elm Grove, Queen's Park and Freshfield Roads. The terminus – Kemp Town Station – seen here (top picture) about 1905, stood off Eastern Road, where the Freshfield Industrial Estate stands today. The tunnel entrance, in the distance on the right, still exists.

Lewes Road Station (opposite), seen in July 1909, with a Sunday school outing about to take place (probably to Hassocks or Burgess Hill), stood on the line at the western end of the Lewes Road viaduct, on a site behind the present Sainsbury store. There was a covered walkway of steps up from Lewes Road, the end of which can be seen beyond the post and lantern left of centre. The end of the viaduct can also be glimpsed, extreme left.

THE TRAM SYSTEM

The town's electric trams have been glimpsed several times in previous views; it was November 1901 when the system was officially inaugurated, beginning a new era in public transport for Brighton, that lasted for nearly 40 years.

In the main view, rails are being laid at the top of Elm Grove early in 1901. Queen's Park Road runs off to the right. The town's workhouse of 1886-87 (now the General Hospital) is on the right.

Work began on the system in January 1901, when Alderman Sandall, chairman of the tramways committee, screwed in the first nut of rails being laid in Lewes Road, where the tram depot would later be located. Work proceeded rapidly along Lewes Road, southwards, then up

Elm Grove and along Queen's Park Road, the trenches to take the rails all dug by some seventy labourers in a matter of a few days.

Eventually, there were eight routes, each given a letter to denote the area covered – 'B' for Beaconsfield, 'N' for New England Road, etc. The whole nine and a half mile system was eventually completed in July 1904 with, surprisingly, the Brighton station route ('S') being last to open.

The other view shows race-day trams at the top of Elm Grove, a few months after the system had opened. Part of the workhouse wall can be seen on the right. Trams would start carrying adverts, on the panels around the top decking, from July 1902.

FIRST MOTOR BUS

It's hard to imagine the stir caused by this vehicle, the first of Brighton's motor buses, which began operating in December 1902. Seen here in Old Stiene, it was a Milnes Daimler vehicle, registration CD103, with a seating capacity of thirty-four (twelve inside, twenty-two on top). The route was from Castle Square to Hove Street and Sackville Road, via Western Road (where trams did not operate), the full journey costing 2d.

Once they were up and running, there were many complaints about the new buses, particularly the noise they made. Traders in Western Road were being ruined, it was claimed at a council meeting of May 1907, and there was a demand for pneumatic tyres to be made compulsory.

Yet motor vehicles had come to stay. With cars and buses increasingly appearing on the roads, electric light replacing gas, airships in the sky (the one here is over Black Rock in October 1910), the first wireless communication with America and any number of other technological developments, it must have seemed to Edwardians that their era could even surpass the Victorians for discovery and invention. Britain was still the wealthiest country in the world at this time, with huge control over world trade, and the British Empire was firmly in place. But even in the early 1900s, clouds were gathering to blot out the glow of Edwardian pride and complacency . . .

FRENCH VISITORS AT THE ROYAL PAVILION

This seemingly innocuous event – the Comite Republicain du Commerce arriving at the Pavilion in May 1907, for a tour of the town and a banquet – was actually an extremely serious and somewhat desperate political event, one of many staged in the early 1900s to ally Britain with France in an attempt to avert war in Europe.

This visit, and other events like the huge Franco-British Exhibition in London, 1908, were part of the *Entente Cordiale* set up largely at the prompting of King Edward VII. Territorial disputes were dividing Europe, and Britain sought to become on far friendlier terms, initially with France, later Russia, to counter the Triple Alliance of Germany, Italy and Austria-Hungary. The idea – naïve now in retrospect – was that any war in Europe would be negated by the resulting 'balance of power'. The peace held until 1914, but then tensions erupted leading to World War One.

All this was seven years away from the innocent flag-waving bustle seen here. *The Sussex Daily News* gave a large amount of column space to welcome the French, but underlined the seriousness of the visit: 'The maintenance of friendly relations between England and France, whether those relations be political, social or commercial, is one of the most important factors in securing the peace of the world.'

SUFFRAGETTES AND MUNITIONS WORKERS

More political unease would be caused by the rise of the Women's Social and Political Union (the Suffragettes), founded by Emmalene and Christabel Pankhurst, in 1903. The group mounted a campaign of civil disobedience - taking extreme measures sometimes – to secure more rights for women, particularly the right to vote in Parliamentary elections.

Hardly any photographs exist of local suffragettes in action, but this rather poor view shows a solitary member drumming up support outside the school in Rottingdean.

In Brighton, there were rallies and marches, with Hove cricket ground suffering a serious arson attack.

What really advanced the cause of womens' rights was their involvement in World War One, with thousands being employed making munitions. Locally, this took place at the Allen West factory in Lewes Road; workers here are seen below.

Eventually, at the end of the war, women over the age of thirty were given the vote. In 1928, the age was reduced to twenty-one, the same as men.

VAD DETACHMENT AT THE STATION

When World War One finally broke out, in August 1914, initial concern and surprise (after all, the Kaiser was the King's cousin) were soon displaced by a manic, patriotic fervour; thousands of men volunteered to fight and all kinds of war work erupted in towns and villages throughout the country, to aid the war effort.

In Brighton though, for many people, particularly the wealthy visitors, the war eventually became an 'out of sight, out of mind' event, which the gaiety of the town served to mask still further. At one point, even the *Brighton Gazette* was asking: 'Is there a war on?', such was the dilution of

concern. A surprising question, when sounds of shelling could be heard from the hills above Brighton and the town was host to thousands of wounded soldiers, many arriving within a month of war starting.

This is the subject of these photographs. Due to the close proximity with northern France, many hospitals along the south coast were used to take men transferred back to Britain from field and base hospitals on the Western Front via Dover, Southampton and Eastbourne. As places would be limited, a large number of other buildings were requisitioned by the authorities and turned into temporary military hospitals. The Brighton, Hove and Sussex Grammar School, in Dyke Road (left), would become one of these, its official name being the 2nd Eastern General Hospital. In the main picture, taken at Brighton Station, men of the 53rd Voluntary Aid Detachment await trains bringing the latest wounded arrivals to the town.

WOUNDED SOLDIERS AT THE GRAMMAR SCHOOL

From the station, it was a straightforward drive to Dyke Road and the converted grammar school. War had been raging for only a month, yet the number of initial casualties to arrive, in September 1914, was 300. These were men of the 2nd Royal Sussex Regiment, involved in the retreat from Mons. There were some 500 places at the hospital, so after this first intake, it was already over half full.

Eighteen doctors, a matron, plus a large number of nurses, nearly all local, were on duty, with the school's laundry becoming the X-ray room. Beds came from the school itself, the workhouse in Elm Grove, Roedean School, plus donations from local people.

In these pictures, eager crowds jostle to see the first intake. Women, in particular, were shocked to see young men, some not much more than boys, limbless, blinded or with other dreadful injuries.

Other places used as hospitals included the school in Stanford Road, St Mark's School in Arundel Road, the John Howard home in Kemp Town, 6 Third Avenue, Hove, and 38 Adelaide Crescent, Hove, Mrs Barney Barnato's house.

INDIAN PATIENTS AT THE PAVILION

When Belgium was overrun and the German army advanced across north-east France towards Paris, the initial force sent by Britain was comparatively small. The urgent need for trained and experienced troops led to soldiers of the Empire's Indian Army being offered for service. They arrived at the Western Front from October 1914, and there were immediate casualties of course. These were also sent to the temporary hospitals along the south coast, many being treated in the New Forest area.

King George V suggested the Pavilion Estate would be an ideal place in Brighton to house wounded Indians. Royal suggestions were always taken up, so 724 beds were installed in the Dome, the Corn Exchange and the Royal Pavilion itself, soon supplemented, due to demand, by 2,000 at the workhouse in Elm Grove, and 550 at the Pelham Street Schools.

The first arrivals were in December 1914. Sanitary and catering provision were very problematic. Animals for meat dishes had to be ritually killed, separate water taps for Hindus and Muslims were installed and the bodies of the Hindu dead had to be cremated with full ritual and ceremony on ghats, set up on the Downs above Patcham.

There was also the 'novelty factor' of having thousands of Indians in the town and an extremely curious public was desperate to see these 'men of the Empire'. A high wall was built round the Pavilion and the best glimpse of the Indians was for 2d from the top of a passing tram.

PAVILION HOSPITAL AND YMCA ANNEXE

In late 1915, the Indian Army was withdrawn from the Western Front and reassigned to the eastern Mediterranean. This meant that from January 1916, the Pavilion hospital buildings were gradually vacated and converted to make way for limbless British soldiers. The first were admitted from April that year, the number of beds being reduced to 526.

Some of the men are seen on the Pavilion lawns taking part in a hairdressing competition. All manner of amusements and diversions were provided for 'the boys', and it is moving to see them laughing and enjoying themselves while having recently lost a limb. Others pose outside the YMCA building in Old Steine, which was used as an annexe to the hospital. It has been extended with a temporary wooden structure across its frontage. From this and a very large prefab-style building in the Pavilion grounds, soldiers were given training in car mechanics, electrical engineering, carpentry and commercial skills, such as typing. 'There is an average daily attendance of 80,' stated a brochure published by the hospital in 1917, 'and the training is already having the satisfactory effect of equipping the students with a practical knowledge that is enabling them to occupy responsible positions on their return to civil life.'

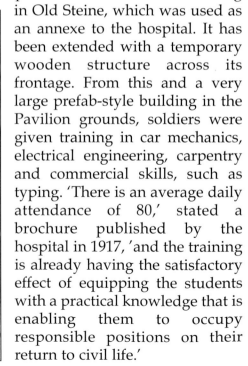

BUILDING THE WEST PIER CONCERT HALL

This photograph of a concert hall being built on the West Pier during World War One, almost gives credence to the notion that Brighton was looking to itself, not the crisis of war in France.

The Palace Pier had opened a winter garden in 1911; this attracted crowds onto the pier, even in poor weather, to hear orchestral concerts. The West Pier responded with its own concert hall, seen under construction here, probably early in 1916. Note the soldiers playing a slot machine, bottom right.

Designed by the local firm of Clayton and Black, the hall opened in April 1916. A Brighton

guidebook of the period states it could hold 1,300 people. It rapidly boosted numbers visiting the pier; in 1920, there were 2,074,000 paying customers – the highest ever in the pier's history.

VISIT OF EARL HAIG

In this view of North Street, November 1920, the flags are out for the visit of Earl Haigh, who would receive the Freedom of the Borough, in recognition of his role as Commander-in-Chief of the British army during World War One. He had already received the Freedom of some fifty other boroughs across the country. When Haigh arrived at the station, a crowd of unemployed men demonstrated (as they were doing in many places at this time), waving a banner stating: 'It's work we want, not charity'; the slump following the war had caused huge unemployment – two million were registered in 1921.

In his speech at the Town Hall, Haigh said: 'I have only one real end in view, the welfare of the brave men who fought so gallantly and so well for the honour and liberty of our country. I have only one object, to see that neither those who died, nor those who were spared to come back to civil occupations are forgotten or overlooked now that their work is done.

'To go over the top time and again, to face the hail of the machine guns, was a very difficult thing. But it was a duty. And it was done. To win the war was a difficult thing. But these men did it.'

UNVEILING THE OLD
STEINE WAR MEMORIAL

In October 1922, on the northern enclosure of Old Steine, Admiral of the Fleet, Earl Beatty, unveiled Brighton's memorial to the dead of World War One. The designer was Brighton-born John W Simpson, president of the Royal Institute of British Architects from 1919 to 1921. The names of 2,600 Brighton people who died in World War One appear on the two pylons flanking the approach to the memorial.

Thirty people fainted at the ceremony. It was described in the *Brighton and Hove Herald*, as an intensely moving,

almost overwhelming event. The hymn *Oh God, Our Help In Ages Past* was sung, with prayers and an address from the Vicar of Brighton, the Rev J Walker Brown. The 'thrilling notes' of the Last Post echoed across the Steine area, with the crowds standing motionless and silent. The most poignant part of the ceremony was near the end, when all the official wreaths had been laid. Unannounced, large numbers of the crowd stepped forward with their own small wreaths and floral tributes, covering every space on the memorial. 'They came on', said the *Herald*, 'till they seemed past counting . . .'

SEAFRONT CROWDS AND TRAFFIC

This photograph, dating from about 1927, shows trippers and holiday makers on the seafront, with traffic building up to a point where cars and having to park them is just starting to cause problems. A four-seater, 8hp Rover at this time cost £190. Despite the slump following World War One, it was

'business as usual' at Brighton where, during the summer months, some five million visitors were arriving by train at this time.

A winter garden now stands on the Palace Pier, opening in April 1912. The Queen's Hotel dates from 1846, but was smaller and originally behind the building seen here on the left, which was then Markwell's Hotel. This was absorbed in 1870, when the Queen's was extended.

Bed and breakfast here, in the 1920s, would cost 10/6d for a single room, per night. At the Grand Hotel, a double room would now be 18/- a night.

THE FISHMARKET

Brighton's fishmarket on the lower promenade is now seen in the 1920s, with motor vehicles replacing most of the horse-drawn carts. The market remained an important source of fresh fish for many hotels, boarding houses and, of course, the town's fish and chip shops.

Traditional methods were still being used by Brighton's fishermen between the wars. Many still made their own nets from cotton-based cordage (there was no nylon at this time) preserved by boiling them in a vat with a

product called 'catechu'. Boats were manhandled into the sea and it was a case of 'all hands to the capstan' to draw the larger ones back up.

The fishing itself followed the seasonal pattern of old, but changes were happening. Engines were slowly replacing sail and the huge boats of the past were being replaced by lighter, smaller craft. Many of the back streets where the fishing communities lived were being demolished under slum-clearance schemes, meaning fishing families had to move to new estates on the outskirts of the town, which played a significant part in the decline of Brighton's fishing industry from the 1930s onwards.

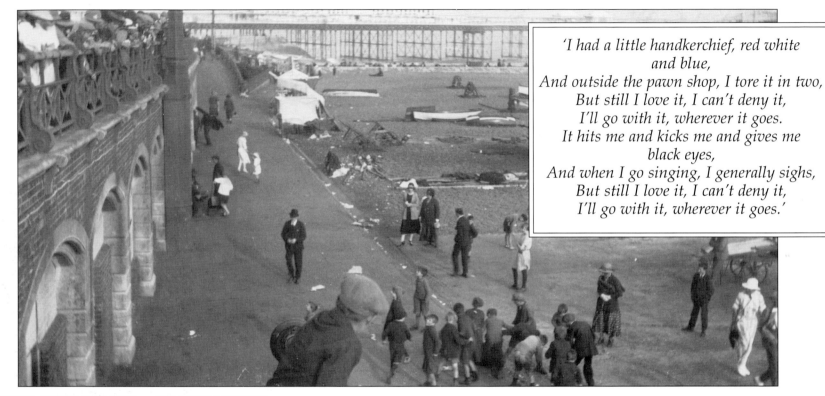

'I had a little handkerchief, red white
and blue,
And outside the pawn shop, I tore it in two,
But still I love it, I can't deny it,
I'll go with it, wherever it goes.
It hits me and kicks me and gives me
black eyes,
And when I go singing, I generally sighs,
But still I love it, I can't deny it,
I'll go with it, wherever it goes.'

LOWER PROMENADE — HAPPYJACKERS

This photograph, another of the seafront in the 1920s, shows poor children known as 'happyjackers', assailing passers-by to throw down coins in return for a song, an action rhyme or burst of acrobatics.

These are all fishermens' children, judging from their 'pitch', the fishmarket hard. Boys and girls from the back streets in the Carlton Hill area touted further east, near the Palace Pier.

Before World War One, happyjacking was mainly begging by chanting loudly. Now the children would perform full songs, mostly music hall favourites, such as 'Daisy, Daisy', but occasionally something more original. The ditty above was passed on by an ex-happyjacker, as an example.

THE REGENT CINEMA

In July 1921, the first – and most would say the best – of Brighton's large-scale 'super cinemas' opened. This was the Regent in Queen's Road, a gloriously original, almost flamboyant building, standing just across the road from the Clock Tower, the site of the present Boots building.

Built in the teeth of the post-war recession, but at the height of interest in motion pictures, it was just the sort of audacious project Brighton could take to its heart. The designer was Robert Atkinson FRIBA, who toured America for three months studying state-of-the-art cinemas there, prior to designing the Brighton Regent. The final cost of the building was more than £400,000, an unbelievable sum for any entertainment building in 1921. Part of this went on massive excavations to provide an underground dance hall – which eventually was abandoned and subsequently added to the roof.

It was a close run thing to get everything ready in time for the cinema's opening. The press reported that the operating licence was delivered at 10.55am (the building opened at 11am) and the pay box was fixed in position two minutes before the doors were opened. All good stories to whip up interest in the new cinema!

INSIDE THE REGENT CINEMA

Two early 1920s views, showing the Regent's sumptuous décor. Initially, the seating capacity was to be 2,200, but this was increased to 3,000. Ticket prices ranged from 9d and 1/- for the stalls, 2/- and 3/6d for circle and balcony, with boxes to seat twelve costing £3. Other boxes seating eight and six were £1/11/6d and £1/5/0d.

The decorative proscenium arch was the work of a local man, Lawrence Preston, of the Municipal School of Art in Grand Parade.

The hyperbole the press threw about to stress the magnificence of the building is typified by this example: 'The Regent is a place of high-class entertainment, in which cheerfulness, good taste, character and luxurious comfort are happily blended. It is dedicated to lovers of wholesome amusement, to people who lead busy lives and who in their leisure hours seek that form of relaxation which brings mental and bodily relief from the days burden of petty worries . . .'

DANCING AT THE REGENT BALLROOM

The Regent Dance Hall opened on the roof of the cinema in December 1923. The photograph shows a 1920s Trafalgar Day dance; Nelson's victory was celebrated in the past far more than it is today.

There were a number of reasons for the rise of dance halls, like the Regent and Sherrys in the inter-war years. Dancing was a joyous reaction following the horrors and carnage of war, and women's emancipation, after working in the munitions factories and other

wartime occupations, meant they no longer had to be chaperoned everywhere and dance halls were the ideal opportunity for 'boy to meet girl' – in fact the Regent was dubbed 'Brighton's marriage bureau' because so many couples met there.

The picture cannot do justice to the hall's lavish décor. The colour scheme consisted of yellow, crimson, blue and purple motifs, blended in all kinds of bizarre patterns, set off by richly-coloured, bell-shaped lanterns. It had a sprung floor, enclosed within a glass-fronted balustrade, which was lit up from within by lights that kept changing colour.

Professional partners could be engaged for 6d a dance, or 15/- for a full afternoon session, or £1 for the evening. Surprisingly, the Regent had no licence at first; dancers could buy only teas and coffees for refreshment.

CHARABANC OUTING

In sharp contrast to the gaiety and affluence suggested by the last picture, is this view of a pub outing departing from near the bottom of Carlton Hill. Although it is the same period, the children on the left could be from Victorian times, with their bare feet and ragged clothing. Here, customers of the Star pub, at 95 Carlton Hill, are

going on a charabanc outing, probably to a country park for the day. Like many pub outings at this time, it was a men only affair. The women have come to see the men off. The vehicle is parked by the Victoria Gardens; the original Municipal School of Art is in the background.

The picture epitomises the living conditions and social life of Brighton people occupying the congested streets of mean housing between Edward Street and Albion Hill. This was considered the main slum area of Brighton, where few visitors would venture.

RICHMOND STREET AREA

At the 1921 Census, when the population was 142,427, the density of people living in Brighton was second only to London's West Ham. The view on this page (of exactly this time) shows why. These are the rows of back streets thrown up from the 1800s onwards as a 'quick fix' to the expanding town's housing needs.

A slum clearance Act of 1930 gave Brighton Corporation a green light to begin demolition of the area on the grounds of poor sanitation, dampness and disrepair resulting in a huge number of displaced families; these were rehoused in new council estates at Whitehawk and Moulscoombe.

Overcrowing wasn't the only problem at this time. Despite all that has been shown so far, Brighton was stagnating during the first quarter of the century. Traffic build up meant extensive road widening was essential, requiring unprecedented clearance work in many streets. Other areas, including the seafront, were shabby and rundown. Massive investment and huge imagination were suddenly needed to pull Brighton firmly into the twentieth century . . .

CREATION OF GREATER BRIGHTON

If one event could be said to have lit the fuse to Brighton's future prosperity at this time, it would be the creation of 'Greater Brighton' in 1928. If one man had to be identified as having been most instrumental in bringing this event about, it would be Sir Herbert Carden

He had been Mayor of Brighton during World War One, and was a dynamic, charismatic councillor with the ability to make snap decisions that were usually right.

Out of his own pocket – he was immensely wealthy – he bought huge areas of Downland surrounding the town, including the Devil's Dyke and Hollingbury estates, thus preventing development by outsiders. Operating as a private individual, he obviously secured a much lower price than if Brighton Corporation had put in bids for it. Then he sold the land to the corporation, at the price he had initially paid, for development in ways best suited to the needs of the town.

This bold dealing and massive acquisition of land enabled the boundaries of Brighton to be vastly extended in May 1928, creating 'Greater Brighton'.

Between 1895 and 1936 Carden bought 12,000 acres of land in this way, for the benefit of the town, at a cost of £800,000. Because of his foresight, magnanimity and unceasing interest in Brighton's development, he is known as the 'Father of Modern Brighton'.

Carden received the Freedom of the Borough in 1926, and was knighted in 1930. He died in 1942.

CREATION OF GREATER BRIGHTON

These two maps, reproduced from the 1924 and 1928 Ordnance Survey editions, show how the boundary line of Brighton suddenly jumped in May 1928, with the creation of Greater Brighton. This was mainly as a result of huge areas of Downland being bought by Sir Herbert Carden, as detailed on the previous page.

Rottingdean, Ovingdean, Patcham, part of Falmer, North Moulscoombe, Hollingbury Camp and golf course, plus the Chattri area (where a memorial to the Indian dead of World War One had been built) all now came within the borough boundary, bringing huge changes to local government.

The area of Brighton increased five times from 2,632 acres to 12,490. The town boasted it was the same size as Chicago. The seafront was now six miles long – previously it had been two and a half. Such expansion had never happened before, and nothing similar would happen again until the town's amalgamation with Hove in April 1997.

GREATER BRIGHTON CELEBRATIONS

This is the cover of a 40-page programme listing the huge number of events staged to celebrate the creation of Greater Brighton.

A whole week of festivities was arranged between 28th May and 2nd June 1928. There were band concerts, firework displays and beacon fires lit at Rottingdean cliffs, Devil's Dyke and Hollingbury Camp.

Other events included gala shows at the theatres and cinemas, 2,500 children 'beating the bounds' of the new borough, a pageant in Preston Park showing the history of Brighton, a World's Fair in the grounds of the Royal Pavilion, opened by Princess Beatrice, plus a civic banquet, with the Lord Mayor of London and Home Secretary William Joynson-Hicks, as guests of honour. Tickets for this were 30/-.

But undoubted highlight of the week was the royal visit by the Duke and Duchess of York, on 30th May.

ROYAL VISIT TO CELEBRATE GREATER BRIGHTON

A motorcade at the Clock Tower passes a banner proclaiming 'Welcome To Greater Brighton'; the beginning of the royal visit by the Duke and Duchess of York (later King George VI and Queen Elizabeth). This was the main event of celebrations marking the extension of the town's boundaries in 1928.

The itinerary for the Duke and Duchess included unveiling a stone seat at Devil's Dyke (still there today) and dedicating a new wing of the children's hospital, the Royal Alexandria, in Dyke Road. They also visited a horse show at Preston Park.

In the photograph, on the left, Burton's store is nearing completion – the first new building in the redevelopment and widening of West Street, begun in 1925.

THE PYLONS — LAYING THE FOUNDATIONS

The first and main duty of the Duke and Duchess of York, when visiting Brighton for the Greater Brighton Celebrations, was to lay the foundation stones for two huge pylons, one on either side of the London Road, close to the new northern boundary of the town.

The main view shows the Duke tapping one stone into place; the Duchess would lay the other. Notice the caps of the workers, duly removed, on the right, plus the scaffolding, which at this time was wooden.

The pylons were designed by John Denman FRIBA, and executed in clipsham stone, as was the seat at the Dyke, which was unveiled in the afternoon.

Today, the pylons still stand, but one is displaced and is in the middle of the London Road, due to the recent building of a new carriageway to facilitate traffic exiting from the Brighton bypass, heading for Gatwick and London.

THE RAILWAY WORKS

Before leaving the 1920s period, a look at part of Brighton's industrial past, an aspect of the town's history that is often ignored.

This 1920 view across Preston Circus and New England Road, shows a section of the extensive locomotive works that stood north of the station. Here was the town's 'heavy' industry, where huge railway locomotives were designed and built; in 1891, 2,651 staff were employed here, turning out twelve engines a year. The works covered a massive site, housing many different depots, stores and

workshops to serve the various stages in production. Power was supplied by an on-site electrical generating plant, but four steam engines were also used, one of which drove the machinery in the sawmill and carpenters' shop, seen in the interior view.

From 1889, the locomotive superintendent was R J Billinton. D Earle Marsh succeeded him in 1905 and the last superintendent was L B Billinton (R J's son), from 1911.

The house in the foreground of the main view, at 74 London Road, was once owned by Henry Longhurst, who ran a brewery where the Preston Circus fire station stands, on the opposite side of the road. His house became a branch of Lloyds Bank in 1924, but was demolished when the corner was rounded off to ease traffic flow in 1935.

NEW ENGLAND ROAD – RAILWAY WORKERS

Railway workers are seen leaving at the end of a shift, probably an early morning one, judging by the shadows. Many lived in the streets nearby. A White's Early Coffee House stands on the corner of Argyle Road. The cast-iron bridge dates from 1852, when a line was built over the road, taking goods traffic to an extensive yard at the top of Trafalgar Street. The tram route – 'N' – began operating just after Christmas, 1901. Although this crowded scene seems to indicate prosperity, from the turn of the century the works were actually in decline, due to redistribution of work to other areas, initially Newhaven and Lancing, later Ashford and Eastleigh. By the 1930s, only repair and maintenance work was undertaken at the Brighton works – although there was renewed activity for a short period from 1942 due to the war effort.

MIDDLE STREET — THE FRYCO WORKS

More of Brighton's industrial past is seen in this extensive factory on the western side of Middle Street, opposite the Hippodrome, in the heart of the Old Town area.

Dating from 1874, it was owned by the firm of

R Fry and Company, who manufactured soft drinks (then called mineral waters), vast quantities of which were needed by the hotels, cinemas and theatres, shops, pubs and piers in the town. In fact there were two Fryco factories in Brighton; the other was in Park Crescent Place, at the northern end of the Level.

The premises here extended through to West Street and were bounded to the north by Boyces Street, where a large set of doors still exist with the sign 'Mineral Water Factory' above them, seen in the smaller view.

In its day, like other factories and breweries in the town, this firm must have employed a considerable number of people. Fry's shut down its Brighton operations in 1930 and moved to Portslade. A large garage presently occupies the Middle Street site.

ELECTION RESULT

The year 1924 saw Britain's first Labour government formed, under Ramsay MacDonald. This interesting postcard was issued in October that year, showing the General Election results for Brighton. In the days before television and when wireless was in its infancy, results in Brighton were issued in postcard form and displayed from a scaffolding rig outside the Corn Exchange, Church Street.

Apart from a few Liberal MPs in the early 1900s, the Conservatives swept the electoral board for most of the century, until Dennis Hobden's legendary win for Labour in October 1964. He won by just seven votes, after seven recounts of the voting papers. This was the only Sussex seat ever won by Labour up to this time, and it was held in the election of 1966, but lost in 1970 to Andrew Bowden.

Major George Tryon (on the right in the picture), was Brighton's longest serving MP, from 1910 to 1940. Cooper Rawson (left), would achieve the highest majority ever, by anyone, at the election of October 1931 – 62,253, over the next contender.

TRYON ▪ 39387
RAWSON ▪ 39253
GORDON ▪ 14072
1924
General Election
Brighton's Conservative Members
Major, Rt Hon. G.C. Tryon & A. Cooper Rawson Esq.
Copy: Fuller & Clayton

▪ 39387
▪ 39253
▪ 14072
The Biggest Polls & the Biggest Majorities. ever recorded in Great Britian.

BRIGHTON PLACE – MOUNTED POLICE

In 1926, the year of the general strike, the Trades Union Congress called for sympathy strikes to support the miners who were threatened with longer hours and a cut in wages. There was great solidarity for the miners and on 4th May Brighton awoke to no trams, buses or newspapers. For nine days – from the 4th to the 12th May, 6,000 workers in the town were on strike.

Brighton's Tramways Committee decided to

train volunteers to drive their vehicles. On 11th May some 4,000 strikers congregated at the Lewes Road depot to prevent trams being driven out. Several hundred police (eighty on horseback) dispersed the crowd, but only after much fighting, many injuries (two serious) and huge ill-feeling.

The photograph here shows the kind of mounted police 'specials', who took part in the 'Battle of Lewes Road', as it has become known, standing in Brighton Place, not far from the Town Hall Police Station. They were also involved in a scuffle and arrests outside the Labour Club in London Road, that day.

On 12th May twenty-two prisoners appeared before the magistrates. Sentences of between one and six months' hard labour were meted out, some to totally innocent men. On the same day, at noon, the general strike was called off and by 2.50pm trams were running again.

THE EASTERN BEACHES — BANK HOLIDAY CROWDS

Our survey of the century moves on to the 1930s, which saw the traditional British seaside holiday peak in popularity, bringing an enormous number of visitors to the town each season.

The view looks down from the Palace Pier, in August 1931. Boat trips seem to be doing good business, and there is the kind of congestion that generated the old variety joke of only bald-headed men getting sunburnt.

In the post-war period, travelling abroad would become affordable for many, taking trade away from local resorts, and crowded beaches swarming with bucket and spade holidaymakers throughout the holiday season would become a thing of the past.

In 1960, for example, Spain would record some six million visitors. In 1970, it was twenty-four million, and by 1990, the figure was fifty-two million.

WIDENING OF WESTERN ROAD

Fired up by the 1928 expansion and the urge to show that Brighton was forward thinking and serious about modernising itself, the 1930s were a startling period of change for the town, both centrally and on the newly-created outskirts.

Sir Herbert Carden urged radical and widespread redevelopment of many areas, particularly the seafront, envisaging that 'Brighton – The City Beautiful', should rise and expand on the cliffs between the Adur at Shoreham, and the Ouse at Newhaven, becoming 'the finest residential city in the world'.

Clearing old property to widen the main roads of the town, then lining them with new state-of-the-art buildings, was seen as making a start on all this.

Western Road, being widened here at its eastern end, in August 1934, was one of these roads. The glass roof of the Imperial Arcade –

originally built in 1924 – has been exposed. At the turn of the century, it had been possible to find a private house with a front garden in among the shops being cleared on this site. The buildings on the southern side of Western Road (left), would come down in 1967 for the first Churchill Square development, widening the road an enormous amount at this point.

WIDENING OF NORTH STREET

A large section of North Street was similarly widened a few years later.

The main photograph shows the northern side in 1937, looking across from Ship Street to property between King Street and Windsor Street. Hoardings show buildings about to be demolished.

The other view, of September 1938, looking west, shows the site clear.

The new building line would be set back, with the Imperial Theatre built at the corner of Windsor Street. Later it became the Essoldo and more recently was the Hotshots entertainment centre, which went bankrupt early in 1999. Barclays Bank would build their distinctive white building at the corner of King Street (now King Place), but not until the 1950s, rebuilding being interrupted by World War Two. Further widening of North Street, lower down, took place in the 1960s.

WIDENING OF WEST STREET

The widening of West Street had begun in November 1925, when a large shop at the top western corner, adjoining North Street (seen on page 10), was cleared and the Burton building rose on the site three years later.

Work then progressively moved down the street, on the western side only, towards the seafront, the final clearance being made at the beginning of 1963, with the demolition of a large hotel near the King's Road corner. Again, the huge time taken was because the war and subsequent slump halted work for a number of years.

The bulk of the demolition and rebuilding work took place in the

1930s, though. The views here both date from April 1931. Above, the upper part of the street has been widened and rebuilt, with the Burton building on the right. Opposite, the lower third of the street is at its old width, awaiting clearance.

SS BRIGHTON IN WEST STREET

This is one building everyone will be expecting to see in this book!

Opened first as a swimming pool in June 1934, the SS Brighton stadium was built on the western side of West Street, following the widening seen on the previous page. The Quality Hotel presently stands on the site.

Its pool was hailed as 'the largest sea-water bath in the world', but it was not a success, despite its prime location and long opening hours – 8am until 10pm. The photograph shows why. Superb weather meant that everyone bypassed the pool and headed straight for the sea, where they could swim free of charge. Accordingly, attendances were poor enough to make the management close the pool and convert the building into an ice rink.

THE SS BRIGHTON SWIMMING POOL

The 1934 photograph on the facing page shows the shallow end (the western part of the building), with painted-on swimmers. The other view is of the diving platforms at the deep end. The pool measured 65ft by 165ft and the interior décor was detailed to make the pool look as if it were on an ocean liner, giving it a luxurious image.

A *Brighton Herald* report of the opening said:

'Under brilliant auspices, the S.S. Brighton – the superb £80,000 swimming stadium in West Street – was 'launched' by Commodore Earl Howe.' As well as swimming and diving displays, a highlight of the opening ceremony was an illuminated model of the Queen Mary liner being towed round the pool.

THE SS BRIGHTON SKATING RINK

The skating rink was opened in October 1935. The building's SS title, which many people took for 'swimming stadium', easily modulated to 'skating stadium'. The rink was 175ft by 75ft and built over the swimming pool on supports fixed directly to the pool floor.

The rink was a huge success, even more so when a new kind of entertainment on ice, called *Viennese Memories*, with fourteen female dancers dressed in amazingly ridiculous costumes, was staged on New Year's Eve, 1936. It proved so popular, that a full-scale show – seen here – played the following summer.

This was *Marina*, the first of many themed ice shows to be held over the years at the SS Brighton; the tradition of these carries on today with the annual *Holiday On Ice* show each winter at the Brighton Centre.

BLACK ROCK POOL

A spate of swimming pool building took place in many resorts across the country during the 1920s and 1930s. Many were in the form of outdoor lidos, in art-deco style, with a café and other facilities on site; somewhere to spend a morning or afternoon – very different from old style municipal baths, where people went for just a quick swim.

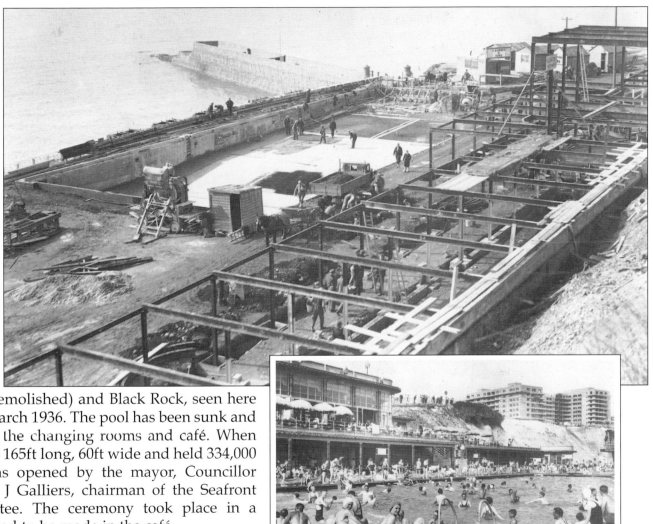

In Brighton three lidos were built, at Saltdean (still there), Rottingdean (recently demolished) and Black Rock, seen here under construction in March 1936. The pool has been sunk and girders are in place for the changing rooms and café. When completed, the pool was 165ft long, 60ft wide and held 334,000 gallons of water. It was opened by the mayor, Councillor Edward Denne, and H J Galliers, chairman of the Seafront Improvements Committee. The ceremony took place in a storm, so the speeches had to be made in the café.

The Marine Gate flats are being completed in the background of the other photograph, making the date of this view 1938.

WIDENING OF EDWARD STREET

More clearance work, in April 1936, for the widening of Edward Street. The corner on the left – seen on page 38 - known as Pavilion Parade, was cleared in 1928 and the Dog Tray pub (the slightly curved building), set back from the other buildings, dates from this time. The picture shows demolition taking place from Sun Street to William Street. Work then proceeded eastwards, up Edward Street, until Riding School Lane was reached in 1946. Slum streets running north from Edward Street were swept away at the same time.

In the 1950s, a large part of the cleared site above William Street became the town's coach park, then the 1960s and 1970s saw remaining property cleared from Riding School Lane right through to Freshfield Road.

All this was done to make Edward Street a dual carriageway which was meant to proceed along Eastern Road to Arundel Road at Black Rock, but it came to nothing, due to Brighton College and the Royal Sussex County Hospital preventing the necessary further widening.

Perhaps the plan was to divert the road to the south of the buildings, but the scheme still didn't materialise and traffic congestion in Eastern Road remains the worst in the area. Did no-one forsee the problems when the plan was put forward ?

CARLTON HILL SLUMS

These two views typify the close-knit network of streets, alleyways and courtyards that proliferated in the Carlton Hill area; removing them was seen as part of the modernisation of Brighton in the enlightened, progressive way that Herbert Carden and his supporters wanted.

The narrow passageway pictured right was near the bottom of Carlton Hill and led to Carlton Court. Three-storey cobble-fronted cottages can be glimpsed in the distance.

The other view is of Carlton Row, running between Carlton Hill and Sussex Street. Both views date from the early 1930s, prior to demolition.

TRAMS AND TROLLEY BUSES

Another huge change was when trams were withdrawn in 1939 and replaced by trolley buses. This followed a town poll on transport issues and a prototype trolley bus being demonstrated on the Level. Trolley buses were seen to be faster, quieter and more modern than trams, but the system didn't change overnight. Trams were phased out from April, trolley buses introduced in June, so for a number of months, both kinds of vehicle were seen, often running alongside each other, as here at the Old Steine terminus.

Once trams had been completely withdrawn, the huge job of taking up the tram rails and scrapping the cars began. Some survived and became chicken coops or outbuildings in various places, but none was fully intact and operative.

During the years the trams had run, the fleet of cars travelled fifty-two million miles, carried 630 million passengers and brought in total revenue of £3,500,000 for the Corporation.

Another important transport change had occurred in 1933, when the main London to Brighton railway line was electrified.

ARMISTICE DAY AT THE WAR MEMORIAL

Crowds gather at the War Memorial in Old Steine for the Armistice Day service of November 1936. During the two-minute silence, at eleven o'clock, the whole country would come to a respectful standstill, to remember the dead of World War One.

World War Two was only three years away at the time of this photograph, giving the scene extra poignancy.

The public's attitude towards Remembrance Sunday, poppy sales and the two-minute silence varied a great deal in the last forty years of the century. Some wanted the whole thing scrapped, others said it should continue being

strictly observed. One mayor of the town, in the 1980's, controversially suggested that white poppies, representing peace, should be sold, instead of the usual red ones. As the century ended however, there was a resurgence of interest and concern. The television coverage of the Falklands War of 1982, and other more recent conflicts, brought home to a new generation the harsh realities of modern warfare. Poppy sales and Remembrance Sunday services continued and the two-minute silence was largely being observed again.

FIGHTER AIRCRAFT OVER THE PALACE PIER

World War One had been fought 'over there', in the fields of France. World War Two would be completely different; this time the town could easily see an invasion force on its beaches and be over-run by the enemy or attacked from the air by bomber aircraft. Civilians would be in the front line just as much as the military.

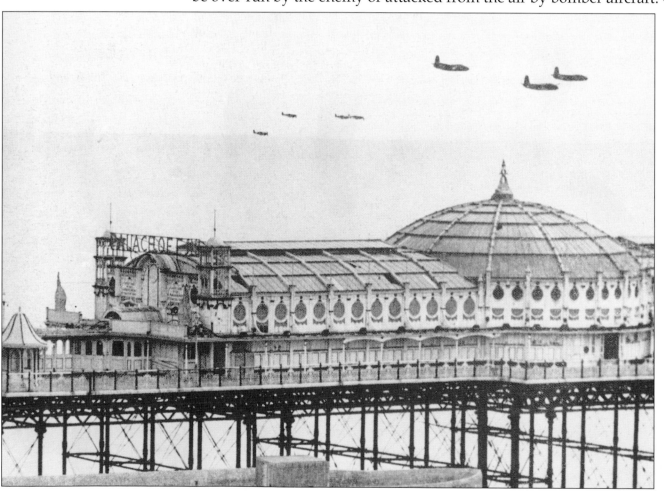

Brighton became a restricted area, with most hotels closed or taken over by the authorities for military purposes. The day after war was declared a huge number of child evacuees – 21,500 – arrived in the town .

The evacuation of the British army from Dunkirk saw 23 ships from Brighton taking part, including two of the Skylark pleasure yachts, some making up to six trips. Two local paddle steamers were also involved, the *Brighton Queen* and the *Brighton Belle*, both of which were sunk.

CENTRAL BEACHES AND LOWER PROMENADE

An amazing picture showing the beaches during World War Two. The West Pier stands with a section removed, to prevent it being used by an invading party. The Palace Pier was the same. The beaches are wired, mined and cleared of boats, many of which went to Sheepcote Valley, above Kemp Town, others to Queen's Park pond. Huge blocks have been positioned at the bottom of the slopes to prevent tanks gaining access to King's Road. These elaborate defences were never tested; attacks on Brighton came entirely from the air.

The date for the invasion of Britain – Operation Sealion – was set for 24th September 1940. Landings would have taken place between Beachy Head and Brighton, with the Royal Pavilion becoming Hilter's HQ in the south, once invasion was secure. But the RAF's victory in the Battle of Britain, in the summer of 1940, saw Sealion indefinitely postponed.

BOMBED AREAS OF KEMP TOWN

What is generally considered Brighton's worst air-raid took place in September 1940, when a single bomber, being chased by a Spitfire, released six or seven bombs over the Kemp Town area. Some 300 people were in the Odeon Cinema in St George's Road when the building suffered a direct hit, resulting in fourteen deaths, many of them children, with another eighty-five seriously injured.

Two more children were killed when another of the bombs fell in Hereford Street, seen above, where a British 'cuppa' seems to be bringing some cheer to survivors.

Altogether, fifty-two people lost their lives from this one raid. Other streets hit were Kemp Town Place, Upper Bedford Street, Upper Rock Gardens and Edward Street.

BOMBING OF MARINE GATE

Due to its prominence and location near the gasometers at Black Rock, the Marine Gate flats (seen under construction on page 81), were bombed and machine-gunned more times than any other Brighton building during the war. This seems to be the attack of April 1942, when a bomb fell close to the flats, shattering a huge number of windows and fatally hurtling a 20-year old woman down a lift shaft.

One of the bombings of Marine Gate is said to have revealed the huge, hidden hoard of a black-marketeer – clothing, whisky and hard-to-get food items. However, this story is told about a great many bombed buildings in Brighton, so possibly it happened, probably it didn't!

The facts and figures of 'the Brighton Blitz', are well known. The first raid was in July 1940, the last in March 1944. There were fifty-six air attacks in all, involving 381 high-explosive bombs and thousands of incendiary bombs (dropped to start fires). There were 198 people killed, 357 seriously injured, and 433 slightly injured. Fatalities in neighbouring towns varied enormously. In Lewes, throughout the whole war, there were only two deaths due to bombing, in Eastbourne, there were 200.

COX'S FACTORY VEHICLES

This photograph was taken to show some of the cars and trade vehicles belonging to Arthur H Cox Ltd, a pharmaceutical factory in Lewes Road. It stood between Upper Lewes Road and the railway viaduct, with its frontage to Lewes Road. A photograph of the factory is on page 100. The vehicles are of interest because they have been modified to be driven during the wartime blackouts. One headlamp is masked on each and the bumpers have been painted white to make the vehicles more conspicuous in the dark. In the background on the left is the covered walkway leading up to Lewes Road Station, seen on page 44. The station stood just beyond the end of the railway viaduct and its roof can be glimpsed on the extreme left. The viaduct was demolished in stages during the 1970s and 1980s, the last section coming down in March 1983.

HOME GUARD DEMOBILISATION

Cheers! Members of a local Home Guard unit toast their stand down, following a final parade in Brighton, December 1944. They are outside the Aquarium Inn, Steine Street, off Brighton's seafront. A radio appeal by Secretary of State for War Anthony Eden, asking for men not in the forces to join Local Defence Volunteer groups, resulted in a huge number of Home Guard units being formed across the country. Nicknamed 'Dad's Army', and later the subject of the immensely popular television series, in Brighton they were primarily used to guard important sites on the seafront, the station area and the Downs above the town.

VISIT OF WINSTON CHURCHILL

Victory in Europe came in May 1945. Church bells rang, bonfires were lit on the beaches and Downs and there was dancing and partying in the streets.

Here, in October 1947, striding purposefully alongside the Mayor of Brighton, Alderman T E Morris, is Britain's great wartime Prime Minister, Winston Churchill, arriving at the Dome having received the Freedom of the Borough, as had Earl Haig and Earl Beatty in the 1920s.

In the 1880s Churchill had attended a preparatory school in Hove run by the Misses Thompson at 29-30 Brunswick Road.

On the day he received the Freedom he attended a luncheon given by the Royal Sussex Regiment, and opened Churchill House in Queen's Road. The following day he addressed the Conservative Party Conference at the Dome. Churchill's last visit to Brighton was in 1952 when he attended the races.

PADDLE STEAMER
BRITTANIA

Although war ended in 1945, the late 1940s and early 1950s still saw hard times. Rationing of some goods continued even more austerely than in the war, due to massive shortages of many food items, coal, tobacco and building materials.

Many families were housed in prefabricated homes set up on bomb sites.

To attract back the pre-war visitors, the beaches were cleared of mines and bulldozed back into shape, the gaps in the piers were restored and everything was done to suggest normality.

Paddle steamer trips had operated from both piers as soon as landing stages had been added. They made trips along the coast to other seaside resorts, to the Isle of Wight, or to France for a day trip. The *Brittania* (or 'Old Brit', as she was nicknamed), is shown in the summer of 1948 or 1949, off the Palace Pier, but only worked two seasons, due to falling holiday trade on the south coast, and was transferred to the Bristol Channel. Her maiden voyage had been in June 1896. She was 230ft in length, 26ft wide and had a top speed of 21 knots. In World War Two, she was a minesweeper known as HMS *Skiddaw*, and took part in the Normandy invasion fleet. She was scrapped in 1956.

DANCING AT THE REGENT

Jiving at the Regent dance hall in about 1957, a view contrasting markedly with the photograph on page 61. The Regent and Sherrys had been the two principal dance halls in Brighton during the inter-war period. But fashions come and go and with the advent of television and pop music from the 1950s onwards, formal dancing became less popular with young people, who preferred to 'do their own thing' to the music of the new, young groups. Jiving, seen here, was a kind of in-between stage in all this.

The Rank organisation had owned the Regent since 1947. With the opening of the Top Rank Suite at the bottom of West Street in November 1965, the Regent's popularity declined, and the famous dance hall closed in July 1967 to became a bingo hall. In November 1970, this became the Big Apple club, where pop concerts were staged.

In April 1973, Rank unveiled its triple-screen cinema in the Top Rank complex (renaming it the Kingswest) leading to the closure of the Regent Cinema the same year.

The cinema and dance hall were demolished in 1974.

THE CURZON CINEMA

The primitive Queen's Electric Cinema, seen on page 27, would survive, in rebuilt and renamed form, for nearly seventy years. This view shows it as the Curzon, in the early 1950s. The first change had come in 1923, when the cinema was renamed the Scala: 'Reconstructed, redecorated, re-seated and re-carpeted', ran the press advertisement. In 1932, it became the Regal then in 1936, the building took the art-deco appearance seen here, becoming the Curzon.

The first advertisement left is for the Curzon's programme of early June 1953. *Elizabeth Is Queen,* is the film for the second part of the week. The coronation of Queen Elizabeth II was the big royal event of the 1950s. The Regent was showing *A Queen Is Crowned*, while the Princes News Theatre, in North Street, had *The Coronation In Colour*, as its main film.

In 1975, with attendances declining, the cinema became the Classic, before closing in August 1979. The site, twenty years later, is covered by the western end of the Waitrose store. At the turn of the century Brighton has four cinemas, the 1910 Duke of York's and three multi-screen complexes. These replace the fourteen cinemas of the inter-war years.

CLOSURE OF THE PALLADIUM CINEMA

Another cinema, but one standing derelict, following closure. This building was seen in all its glory on pages 25 and 26, as the Alhambra theatre of 1888.

It became a cinema in April 1912 and operated successfully, changing frontages first in 1914, then again, in deco style, in 1936.

It closed in 1956. Clearance would come in the early 1960s, for the redevelopment of King's Road between the Grand Hotel and the corner of West Street. Today, the site is covered by the Brighton Centre.

The building on the right here was once part of Muttons hotel and restaurant seen on page 11. Russell Street is where the two people are, on the left.

SHOPPING AT SAINSBURY'S

Food rationing finally ended in July 1954. This view is of Sainsbury's store at 66 Western Road, in 1958. These were the days of polite queuing and marble counters, when quantities of meat and cheese were weighed on huge old-fashioned scales, and butter was cut from a large block, patted with wooden spatulas, then wrapped in greaseproof paper. Payment was always cash – credit cards were unheard of.

All vastly different from today's superstores where the placing of every package is psychologically calculated, where products are precisely lit to make them more attractive and clocks don't exist, so that customers are unaware of how long they are taking to shop.

CLOSURE OF THE FISHMARKET

A photograph taken in November 1957, three years before Brighton's historic seafront fishmarket was forced to close. This scene is very different from those on pages 16 and 57, with far fewer barrows and fish for sale. The council considered the place unhygienic, smelly and outdated and offered new premises in Circus Street, next to the fruit and vegetable market.

The fishermen wanted to stay, but protests, petitions and the asserting of ancient rights came to nothing, and the market was forced to move to Circus Street in 1960.

In October 1972 it was found that there were only three registered boats fishing off Brighton beach. Today, no-one regularly fishes off Brighton and the twenty-five or so fishermen left work from the Marina, Eastbourne or Newhaven. A part of Brighton's historic association with the sea was irrevocably lost when the market closed, and the lower promenade area has never been quite the same since, despite the setting up of a Fishing Museum, left, which opened in May 1994.

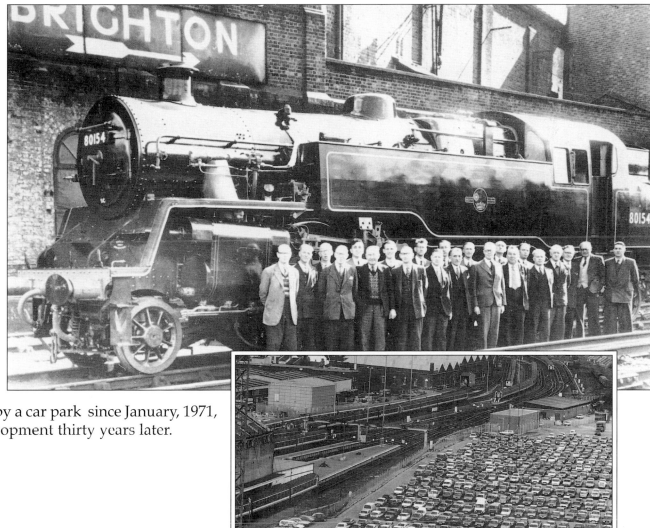

CLOSURE OF THE RAILWAY WORKS

Here, in March 1957, the last locomotive to be built at Brighton is surrounded by the men involved in its production; the works manager, L Granshaw, is seventh from the right.

After being run down intermittently for a large number of years, the works finally closed in 1958. Clearance of the huge site came eleven years later. This area, which has been occupied by a car park since January, 1971, still awaits proper redevelopment thirty years later.

COX'S PILL FACTORY

This huge factory stood between the end of Upper Lewes Road and the railway viaduct, facing Lewes Road. The site today is occupied by a Sainsbury superstore.

The firm was founded in June 1838 by Arthur H Cox, who initially operated from a small shop in Ship Street. The firm expanded, and the large factory seen here was occupied early in 1911 (previously it was a laundry).

Cox's manufactured medicinal products, and its main claim to fame was originating the sugar-coated pill.

The Victorian premises were found difficult to modernise and in 1979 Cox's was forced to move to the Whiddon Valley in Barnstaple, Devon.

The factory building was demolished in 1983, seen on page 133.

HELTER SKELTER ON THE PIER

A slide down the Palace Pier's helter skelter brings this look at Brighton over the last century into the decade of the 1960s. It is August 1962. The screams and background noise can almost be heard; all the scene lacks is someone eating fish and chips wearing a 'kiss me quick' hat.

Young people dominate the scene. Two Teddy Boys stand on the left. The picture personifies youth culture at this time and its liberation in the years following World War Two. It's interesting how photographs of Brighton's seafront and piers show social trends and changes more clearly than most other views of the town.

Young people were finding their feet and their voices now, doing more of what they wanted, listening to their own kind of music and going around together without being overseen by adults.

Coffee bars opened to accommodate their socialising, discos for their dancing. By the late 1970s there were some 7,000 disco clubs in the country. The 'generation gap' found further resolution in extremes of fashion, music and drug taking. Young people would accordingly become a massively exploitable commodity in the last quarter of the century, with a whole array of merchandise aimed directly at them – recorded music, clothing and footwear, electrical gadgets and computer games.

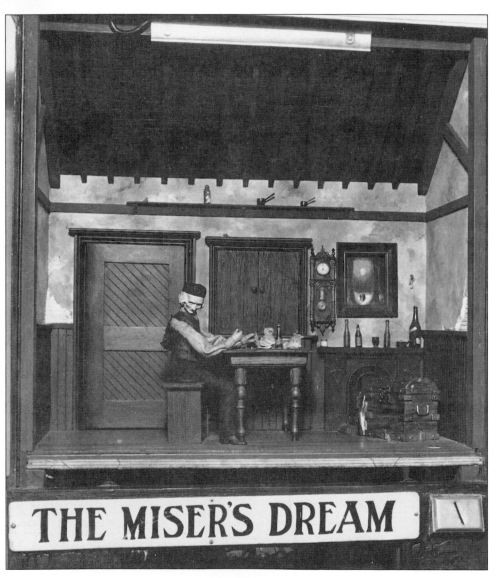

THE MISER'S DREAM

'THE MISER'S DREAM' SLOT MACHINE

The teenagers on the previous page would almost certainly have seen this machine, and others like it, in the Palace of Fun on the Palace Pier. A penny in the slot would bring the scene to clockwork life; doors would open, the picture would slide back and the trunk lid hinge up, revealing all sorts of ghosts and horrors, the miser of course, looking the wrong way each time to see them. After a minute or so, all disappeared and the scene would resume its original state (unless the clockwork had wound down, then it would stop half way through the movement).

There were about a dozen of these machines on the pier, all beautifully made and detailed by Nelson Lee. They were sold off to a private collector in 1971.

A walk through the Palace of Fun today would reveal wall-to-wall slot machines and simulated rides, none of them like the simple pennyworth of fun seen here.

In May 1999, the pier celebrated its centenary, and it was a pity that some of these old machines couldn't have been tracked down and displayed as part of the celebrations.

MEN'S FASHIONS

September 1969 and models pose on the West Pier wearing the latest fashions for men. Left, is what was known as a 'highwayman's raincoat', centre a green-blue paisley suit in Crimpline and right a Kaftan unisex gown. What would the group on the pier pictured on page 18 make of these young men and the way they are dressed?

The West Pier was about to be closed at this time. The seaward end was barred as unsafe in October 1970, then the whole pier was shut down in September 1975. This was due to lack of maintenance and investment following the war, particularly when it was owned by AVP Industries during the late 1960s. The company also owned the Metropole and Bedford Hotels; the latter, seen in the background to the right, opened in September 1967. It replaced the original 1829 building, which was demolished after a fire in April 1964.

Demolition of the pier seemed likely following closure, leading to the 'We Want The West Pier' campaign, led by local shopkeeper, the late John Lloyd. The West Pier Trust, a registered charity, was instigated in 1978.

Many schemes for the pier came and went over the next few years, each one bringing ever increasing estimates for restoration. One of the most promising, in 1988, from Merlin International, was approved by the Trust, but fell through due to the withdrawal of grants by English Heritage. The estimate then was £30 million.

MODS AND ROCKERS

One of the most potent and well-known images of the post-war period in Brighton; the clash between Mods and Rockers on the Aquarium terrace, Bank Holiday Monday, May 1964. Mods are trying to drive Rockers from the terrace under a barrage of deck chairs, some having to drop down over the balustrade to Madeira Drive.

The Mod ideal centred around smart clothing, pop music, dancing and the all-important motor scooter. Rockers wore studded leather gear and chains, liked heavy rock music and rode powerful motorbikes.

Rockers considered Mods to be weak and namby-pamby, and so fair game for a bashing.

In succeeding years, a police ploy to prevent similar incidents was to confiscate Mods' scooters and Rockers' bikes and take them to Devil's Dyke, where they could be recovered, but only after a long, uphill walk.

ROTARY ASSEMBLY AT SS BRIGHTON

SS Brighton (see pages 78-80) was a multi-purpose building where, over the years, all manner of sporting events, shows and meetings were held, including the Rotary Assembly of the early 1960s seen here. Tennis matches, boxing, basketball, judo, snooker, table-tennis and wrestling, political conferences and any number of spectacular ice shows, made it the Brighton Centre of its day. The rink had to be covered for most of these events of course, and sometimes delegates at meetings complained of chilly feet once the coldness of the ice had worked its way through the matting laid over the rink!

BRIGHTON TIGERS

The famous Brighton Tigers ice hockey team is pictured at SS Brighton, having just won a match in January 1965. The Tigers, Brighton's home team, had an enormous following in the town and throughout Sussex. They were British Champions three times – 1946-47, 1947-48 and 1957-58.

The picture here was taken at the final of the Cobley Cup, against Wembley Lions, a very hard fought match. 'After a long run of early victories, Tigers really had to put their heads down and hold on,' said the match report in the *Brighton and Hove Gazette*. The score was 9-8 to the Tigers when a penalty finally clinched the match in their favour. In the picture, Jackie Dryburgh and Rupe Fresher lead the lap of honour. But the Tigers' days were numbered; their last match would be played four months after this picture was taken.

CLOSURE OF SS BRIGHTON

The last event held at SS Brighton was the Conservative Party Conference of 1965, which ran from 13th to 16th October. This picture dates from the 17th October, when the television crew covering the event was moving equipment out. On the left, at the seafront corner of West Street, the Top Rank complex is under construction.

The question of why SS Brighton had to close when it was clearly so enormously popular is often asked. The answer is provided by the model of the proposed Top Rank Centre, photographed in February 1964.

SS Brighton was owned by the Rank group at this time, and part of the group's new entertainment complex was initially intended to cover the site (the section of model on the right), housing shops and a restaurant. Although SS Brighton was cleared for this, the Top Rank building wasn't extended over the site as intended and the area remained as a 'temporary' car park, until the building of the Oak Hotel (now the Quality) in the early 1990s.

DEMOLITION OF SS BRIGHTON
The interior of the ice rink is gutted; a photograph taken in early February 1966. The floor has been taken up revealing the shallow end of the old swimming pool of 1934. Part of the Grand Hotel can be seen top left and the chimney of an old brewery building in Russell Street is on the right.

COMPLETION OF THE
TOP RANK CENTRE

Already described as 'monstrous' and 'an eyesore', while it was being built, the Top Rank building opened in November 1965. The view here shows the exterior nearing completion earlier in the year. The design of the building aroused enormous hostility because it was basically just a concrete box and architecturally at odds with all the other buildings on the seafront, particularly the nearby Grand Hotel. The lack of any detailing, to relieve the monotony of the façade, was particularly criticised, leading later to one large window being installed on the seafront side.

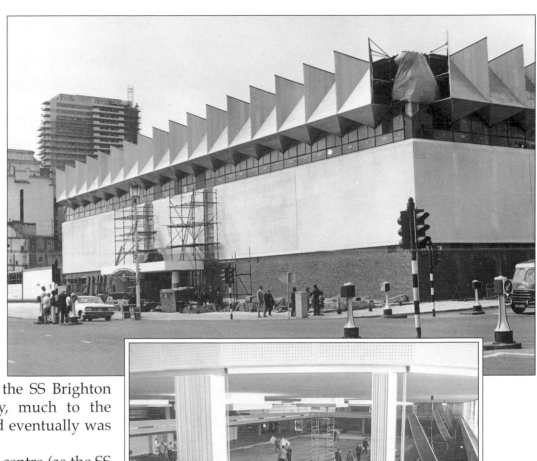

Initially, in 1965, the building housed just a dance hall – the Top Rank Suite – and bar areas, but in December 1966, an ice rink and bowling alley opened. The ice rink was welcomed as a replacement for the SS Brighton one, but was unsuitable for ice hockey, much to the disappointment of Brighton Tiger fans, and eventually was financially unsuccessful.

It could however, double as a conference centre (as the SS Brighton had done), holding some 6,000 delegates. In fact it housed the Labour Party Conference of October 1966; the carpeting for this is seen being laid, right.

SHERRY'S BAR AND ROLLER RINK

Here, the old concert hall building in West Street (seen on page 31), stands as the Ritz Skating Rink and bar, in December 1960. The famous dance hall had closed in September 1948 (it actually re-opened for another year or two), but eventually became a bingo hall, then the roller skating rink seen here.

It was at the peak of its popularity during World War Two; every night it was thronged with all nationalities of allied service personnel.

The building came down in February 1969 and was replaced by a new £150,000 dance hall, its design based on the saloon bar of a Mississippi paddle boat.

As the century turns, the site of Sherrys is occupied by the Paradox night club, so dancing still continues at the bottom of West Street, albeit to the latest techno-beat sound, rather than the melodic ballroom music of old.

LAST CORNER SHOP IN CARLTON HILL

The demise of the small corner shop throughout the post-war period is epitomised by this view of the early 1960s. This grocers at the corner of Carlton Hill and William Street was typical of the scores of small shops that were once common in the area.

For regular customers a 'slate' system often operated, where purchases were listed, put 'on the slate', and paid for when the week was up.

This shop was described by Georgina Attrell in the book *Backyard Brighton*, published in 1988:

'The grocer's shop that I remember best was Corder's. This was like an Aladdin's cave, you took your bottle to buy the vinegar and a jam jar for jam. Everything was loose and had to be weighed and put into thick blue paper bags. Sugar, rice, soda and all the dried fruit came in hessian sacks. We used to buy soap in a long bar, about ten or twelve inches long, and what you required was cut off. Soap was always bought long before you needed it and stored so that it went hard; this way it lasted longer. There was no toilet soap then, you washed and cleaned your house with yellow household soap.'

CONSTRUCTION OF CHURCHILL SQUARE

The photograph on the previous page, from 1965, shows site clearance for the Churchill Square shopping centre. This will be fully described in Volume II, with views of some of the seventeen streets and courtyards that were demolished for the project.

The development plans date from 1929, when the corporation bought land from Sir Oswald Stoll. This was mainly the site of a large brewery, at the bottom of West Street, cleared in 1932. Quite a number of houses were then swept away as slum clearance in the Thirties. As opportunities arose, other old houses and properties came down, but the war put a stop to any large-scale clearance and redevelopment.

In the 1950s, what remained had become very run down, some parts almost derelict, finally leading to the complete redevelopment between Western Road and the seafront during the 1960s and 1970s.

The photograph shows only half of Grenville Place left standing (behind the long hoarding) and beyond, left, the shops of Western Road can be made out. Upper Russell Street ran from the line of buildings at the bottom of the picture, in the centre, diagonally across to the right, then swung northwards past the lines of cars, towards Western Road.

The first Churchill Square would open in October 1968, the recent, rebuilt version in September 1998.

Above, is the Cannon Brewery in Russell Street, photographed in 1968. Nothing here now exists. Final clearance of Russell Street came in May 1969, for the last stage of the Churchill Square/Brighton Centre development; in fact top right, in the distance, the 'Spirit of Brighton' sculpture, a feature of the original square, can be seen in place.

The view is dominated by the old Cannon Brewery of 1821. This started in a small way in the Russell Street home of John Barnett who, before building his brewery, sold his home brew round the town on a cart. Successive owners built trade up until the brewery owned fifty pubs. Tamplins took over in 1926, but ceased brewing three years later, the building becoming a bottling plant. Final closure came in 1965, following a compulsory purchase order. With its long history, the brewery existed for 150 years – another example of Brighton's important industrial past.

CLOSURE OF THE HIPPODROME

The Hippodrome stands empty, following closure in October 1965. The last week's show was given by the Molseyev Dance Company of Russia, followed by the second Beatles concert a week later. The impact of television affected most variety theatres during the late 1950s and early 1960s, and in Brighton some had to convert into cinemas to survive (like the Imperial in North Street, which became the Essoldo, and the Grand in North Road), others to bingo, like the Hippodrome. Live variety shows had had their day and although big star names would continue working, supporting acts dwindled away and theatres struggled to find acts to make up shows for fifty-two weeks in the year.

A deal – with Charles Forte – to turn the theatre into a £250,000 'Talk Of

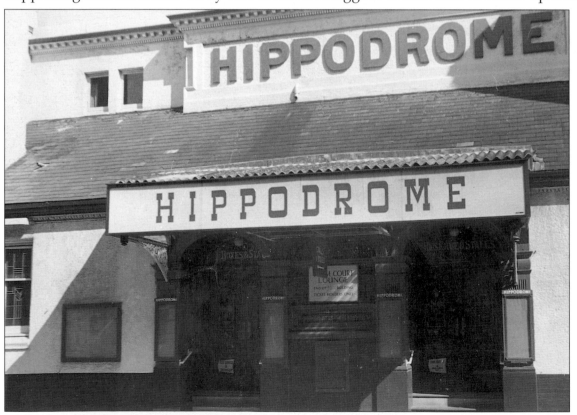

The Town' night-club, fell through. The theatre was adapted to a television studio early in 1966, but this venture was short-lived. Several well-known performers appeared though, including Dusty Springfield, the pop group Freddie and the Dreamers, and American singing star, Liza Minnelli, daughter of Judy Garland, seen here.

MAX MILLER

Brighton's own 'cheeky chappie', Max Miller, is pictured, in the autumn of 1960, at his home at 25 Burlington Street, where he had lived since 1948.

Miller, real name Thomas Sargent, is generally considered the best stand-up comedian of his generation. His material, packed with 'naughty but nice' innuendo and his loud, floral suits were completely at one with Brighton's racy image.

The smaller view shows him (centre, standing) when he was beginning his professional career in 1919, with Jack Sheppard's entertainment group on the seafront and West Pier. He went on to appear as principal comedian in Tom Arnold's show, *Piccadilly* in 1926 and in time became one of the highest paid performers in the business, appearing in three Royal Variety shows (1931, 1937 and 1950) and making a number of films.

By the early 1960s, due mainly to television, variety was dying and so were its stars. Miller's last stage appearance was in December 1960. In May 1963, he died, at the age of sixty-nine.

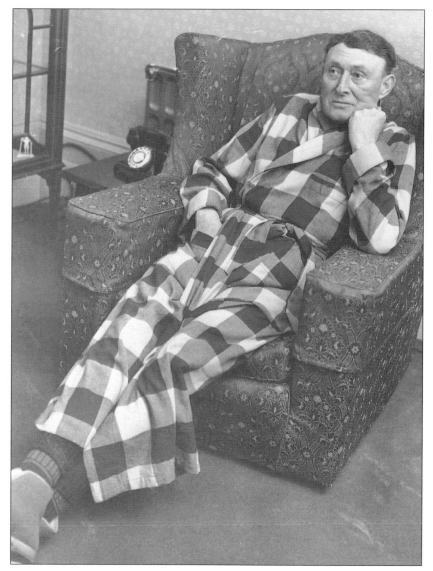

BRIGHTON MARINA PROPOSAL

For the best part of 200 years there had been proposals for some kind of harbour at Brighton, but the basic problem of siting and engineering a structure that would, essentially, stand in the open sea, proved to be too daunting or too expensive until the post-war period.

From 1963, following ideas put forward by Henry Cohen – a Brighton garage proprietor and keen yachtsman – some twelve years of enquiries, site changes, town polls,

Parliamentary Bills and ever-escalating costs took place before the Brighton Marina at Black Rock took shape.

The photograph here shows a model of the marina which appeared in a publicity brochure prepared in 1965. The smaller view is an artist's impression of how the entrance would look. At a cost of £9 million, as well as berths for several thousand boats, it was to have many attractions and features, including an oceanarium, sports centre, open-air tennis courts, an ice rink, fishmarket, several public houses and a fifty-bedroom hotel, plus a large amount of residential accommodation, in order that the marina would 'live 12 months of the year and not become dormant in the off-season'.

It was the new road system needed to access the site that caused most of the stumbling blocks once the main idea had

been accepted. Many groups lodged formal objections, including the Quakers, whose small burial ground next to the gasometers at Black Rock, had to be cleared.

OPENING OF BRIGHTON MARINA

The building of the marina was probably the most significant event in Brighton during the 1970s. This 1975 aerial view of part of the marina site shows the slip roads, tunnels and main interchange of the project in place. The construction firm was Taylor Woodrow.

In the centre is the huge casting yard, where 110 cassions were formed, on site, to create the outer breakwaters, or main walls of the marina. They were each thirty-eight feet high, forty feet across and weighed 600 tons. When in place they were filled with 1,000 tons of concrete. The last one was positioned in April 1976.

Peter Best, the Mayor of Brighton, inaugurated the lock gates between the inner and outer harbours, in May 1977, and the public was admitted from July 1978. The marina was officially opened in May 1979, by the Queen, seen here with the Duke of Edinburgh at the unveiling. The cost had been £41 million, and the final version bore no resemblance at all to any early proposal, such as the one on page 116.

OPENING OF THE BRIGHTON CENTRE

Prime Minister James Callaghan is greeted by protesters at the opening of the Brighton Centre in September 1977. This building completed the redevelopment site between Western Road and the seafront begun in the 1920s. The Grand Hotel was originally to be demolished as part of this scheme, but protests saw the hotel become a listed building, blocking its removal.

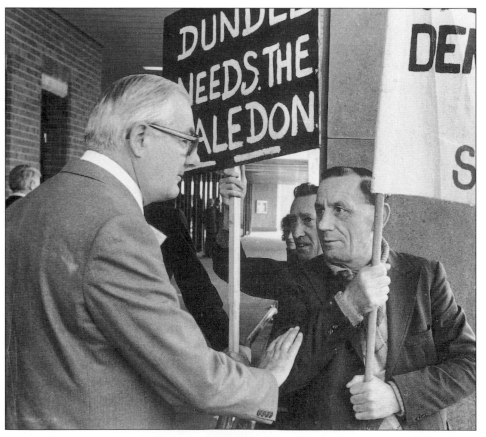

With the centre up and running, Brighton sought to become the top conference town in the country, to promote itself as an up-market, fashionable resort, rather than a tripper town. Over the next twenty years huge investment would be made, in phases, to smartening up the seafront.

Despite its first-rate facilities, the Brighton Centre building has been described as 'ponderous' and 'big and boring', while a guide to the buildings of Brighton, published a few years after the centre opened, said: 'What a pity that, along with its neighbour the Kingswest building, it could not have been handled architecturally with more wit and with less regard for the panorama of King's Road'.

SQUATTER PROTESTS

There had been squatting in Brighton during the 1920s, when Harry Cowley, a chimney sweep, led a vigilantes group, taking over old property in the town to house homeless families, and establishing himself as a champion of the poor. Here, decades later, in May 1974, a cascade of flour bombs shower down over police and bailiffs trying to evict a family of six from council-owned property in Terminus Road. On the day of eviction, they barricaded themselves behind furniture, while demonstrators pelted the officials with flour, sand, coffee and water from the windows. One demonstrator chained himself to the front door and bailiffs vainly sought to remove him with bolt-cutters.

Squatting was common during the 1970s and 1980s in Brighton.

The other photograph shows a squatter at the door of The Coachman's Arms in Trafalgar Street, taken over in June 1988. The young man here wouldn't have looked out of place in the photograph on page 62, taken sixty years earlier. Poverty everywhere continued, right through to the end of the century.

FIRE AT JOHNSON BROTHERS

A photograph of the fire at Johnson's furniture store in November 1970. It was thought to be started by a firework (the fire was on the morning after November 5th) setting light to a pile of rubbish. The resulting blaze was discovered by a patrolling policeman, who saw smoke coming from the building at 2.45am. Seventy fire-fighters from both East and West Sussex brigades fought the fire, taking nearly three hours to bring it under control.

The gutted building was demolished, the firm continuing to trade from temporary premises in London Road. The business eventually moved back to a smaller building on the old site, but closed down in February 1979. The building today is largely occupied by C and H Fabrics, which formerly was in Churchill Square.

Johnson Brothers had started as a single shop in 1902, founded by brothers H Bertram Johnson (then aged only eighteen), and James.

GROUNDING OF THE *ATHINA B*

The top sightseeing attraction in Brighton during 1980 was this cargo ship, the *Athina B*, beached in January that year, east of the Palace Pier, roughly in line with Lower Rock Gardens.

The ship had sailed in December, with a cargo of pumice, from the Azores, via La Rochelle, to Shoreham Harbour. The Captain lost steerage at the harbour entrance and the ship drifted away eastwards, in rough seas. The crew had to be taken off by the Shoreham lifeboat, the Coxswain, Ken Voice, later receiving the RNLI silver medal for his skill and bravery in saving twenty-five lives.

The ship ran aground at Brighton on 21st January, fortunately missing the Palace Pier, where crowds flocked to see it. She stayed on Brighton beach for the best part of a month, finally being re-floated on 17th February.

At Chatham the ship was scrapped, but the anchor was given to Brighton and is presently displayed on Madeira Drive, opposite the Athina Beach, named after the ship.

A fish and chip shop in Station Road, Portslade, is still, at present, named the Athina B, twenty years after the event, although the spelling is different.

OPENING OF THE NUDIST BEACH

Another beach crowded with sightseers, this time in April 1980. The event is the opening of the first nudist beach in the country, situated below Duke's Mound, Kemp Town. The view was taken on opening day, 1st April! Crowds have turned up to see a handful of nudists who look decidedly uncomfortable, both with the chilly weather and the attention they're getting. Ah well, this is Brighton! The original signs stating 'Clothing Need Not Be Worn' were stolen, many letters of complaint were written to the council and local papers, and the beach was threatened with closure three years after opening. However, a petition to save it was instigated, by cheerful naked campaigners getting names on the seafront, and the nudist beach was subsequently retained.

HURRICANE DAMAGE

In the early morning of Friday, October 16, 1987, southern England was devastated by a hurricane. Winds of more than 100mph were recorded, enormous damage was caused to property and, in Brighton, all the parks had trees uprooted, as here on the Level.

Hurricane-force winds caused damage to thousands of houses, sweeping away fences, roofs and chimney pots, overturning cars and tossing seafront chalets at Hove across the lawns.

On the Level 323 trees were uprooted, with another thirty-seven

so badly damaged that later they had to be felled. This left just 150 of the original number – planted in 1844 – remaining.

The smaller view shows damage to the Royal Pavilion, which was undergoing restoration at the time the hurricane struck. Plastic screening has been ripped to shreds although the building itself suffered very little, structurally. A minaret was dislodged, which crashed through the roof of the music room, damaging a newly-installed carpet.

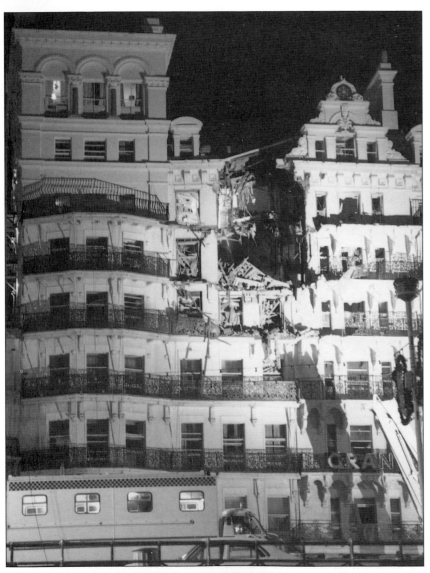

THE BRIGHTON BOMBING

Brighton became headline news throughout the world on 12th October 1984, when a terrorist bomb exploded in an upper storey of the Grand Hotel, killing five people, injuring thirty-four others and damaging a large part of the building.

The bomb was intended to kill the Prime Minister, Margaret Thatcher, and wipe out members of her Cabinet, who were attending the Conservative Party conference at the Brighton Centre that year.

The bomb exploded at 2.45am in room 629, ripping through three of the upper storeys, throwing debris across the street onto the beach and dislodging a rooftop chimney stack weighing several tons. This dropped down through the floors, taking masonry, furnishings and people with it. The hole between the fifth and seventh floors was later the scene of dramatic rescues recorded by television cameras and watched by the whole country on news bulletins. Amazingly, one MP slept through the whole incident. An IRA terrorist, Patrick Magee, was later imprisoned for planting the bomb.

REOPENING OF THE GRAND HOTEL

Margaret Thatcher is photographed at the official reopening of the Grand Hotel in August 1986. With her is Norman Tebbitt, the then Leader of the Conservative Party. He fell through several floors of the bomb-wrecked hotel and had been trapped for four hours.

In the picture, Mrs Thatcher is seen watching Concorde fly past the hotel at the reopening ceremony. The *Evening Argus* reported: 'At one stage it was difficult to know where to look for the best. On one side, Concorde swooped proud and low over the seafront, lights blazing and jet engines pounding the ears. On the other side, within an arm's distance, Mrs Thatcher was clasping her hands in schoolgirl delight and gazing at what was truly a remarkable sight.'

The restoration had cost £11 million, of which only £3.7 million was from the insurance cover. Room 629 was renumbered 621 and the rooms occupied by Mrs Thatcher, the 'Napoleon Suite', became the 'Presidential Suite'.

VOLK'S RAILWAY CENTENARY

In August 1983 the centenary of Volk's Railway was celebrated. Eighty-three-year-old Conrad Volk, youngest son of the line's inventor and builder, waves from the controls. The mayor, Charles Jermy, is on his left.

The great novelty of the line, then and now, is the propulsion method. How do the cars operate? There is, seemingly, no motor unit, the railway is simply cars on rails that glide forward. The answer lies in the wheels, which are driven by electricity; they pick up power from one rail, which drives a small motor propelling the car forward, then returns the power to the other rail. The plant, generating the electricity needed, is housed in an arch on Madeira Drive, opposite the Banjo Groyne, which is where Magnus Volk also had his workshop.

As the century turns, Volk's Railway still operates successfully along Maderia Drive, but many feel the two terminus buildings should be moved to take the line from the Palace Pier into Brighton Marina. This would make the railway go somewhere more definite than it does at the present.

DEMOLITION OF THE
PALACE PIER THEATRE

The Palace Pier Theatre presented summer shows right through to the early 1970s. Variety shows starring Dick Emery, Jack Tripp, Ronnie Corbett, plus the infamous 'Pyjama Tops' show, where naked girls swam around in a huge tank, were among the last to be staged.

The final production was *Music Hall At The Palace*, in 1973, starring old timers Elsie and Doris Walters,

Nat Jackley and Sandy Powell.

The following autumn, a steel barge being used to remove the pier's old landing stages, broke free of its mooring during a storm and repeatedly battered piles under the western side of the pier head close to one side of the theatre. Twenty-five piles sheared off, causing decking and the theatre to drop several feet and the helter-skelter to crash into the sea. Repairs were made at a cost of some £1 million, but the theatre never reopened and for a time housed a display of period slot machines.

The Noble Organisation, which bought the pier in February 1984 for £1.5 million, sought to renovate and update the pier's features. The theatre was demolished in the spring of 1986, with the promise that a new entertainment building would eventually replace it. Currently, a domed amusement arcade occupies the site of the old theatre.

REDEVELOPMENT OF BRIGHTON MARINA

The main view here, looking eastwards across the Marina, was taken in November 1985. The site is bare and undeveloped; not one of the buildings shown in the photograph on page 116 was built and the marina existed at first purely as a harbour for boats, with none of the attractions it has today.

Redevelopment, seen below, came about when the marina was bought by the Brent Walker company in November 1985, for just £13 million. In January 1986, work began on a £120 million redevelopment programme, which involved reclaiming the inner harbour and building a range of amenities and housing. These included a superstore, which opened in November 1987, followed by the marina village – 762 houses and flats, plus sixty-eight holiday homes, a new, small harbour, shops and a pub.

The village is seen under construction in June 1988. Brent Walker went bankrupt in 1994 and the marina was bought for £9 million by Andrew Goodall, who continued the redevelopment programme. A hotel is planned for early in 2001.

DEMOLITION OF BLACK ROCK SWIMMING POOL

In 1974 the council spent £25,600 renovating the pool at Black Rock, seen on page 81, but four years later, 'shocked' at its condition, decided to close it after the summer season of 1978. Local groups began a vigorous campaign to save the pool, but the council considered the cost of restoring the pool to be prohibitive and wanted the site redeveloped. Among suggestions were building

a motel or using the area as a much-needed lorry park. Local residents favoured a small-scale children's playground.

In November 1983 the council approved an offer from Theme Scheme Leisure Developments which planned to replace the pool with a £4 million water park. The photographs here date from March 1984, shortly before demolition took place. The smaller view is of one of the changing baskets, used for holding clothing while swimmers were in the water. A disc, bearing the basket's number, would be issued (with safety pin) for retrieving it at the end of the session.

Nothing became of the water park idea but, by 1999, several new plans were being considered, including building a skating complex or hotel on the site.

REOPENING OF THE WEST PIER'S ENTRANCE DECK

September 1987; after years of the pier standing closed and derelict, funds finally allowed a tiny part of it to be restored and opened to the public again.

Here, the mayor, Cllr Raymond Blackwood, cuts the ribbon to open the completed entrance section. The cost had been £230,000. With the mayor are some local entertainers known as the Pier Rotters.

The plan now was to site stalls and attractions on the new deck in order to generate revenue for future building.

COLLAPSE OF WEST PIER'S SUB-STRUCTURE

The optimism generated by reopening part of the West Pier, in September 1987, was dissipated when a landslip caused a set of piles near the shore to twist round and tilt. This part of the pier had already been weakened by the great storm of October 1987, when a hurricane caused widespread damage to many buildings in the town. This view, of February 1988, shows how the twisted piles have dragged down a large section of the pier's substructure.

The decision was made to cut away the piles and damaged deck section (some 110ft in length), before the supports collapsed, breaking the pier up. The West Pier Trust had funds available for this, but not for the rebuilding; a large gap would therefore be left in the pier.

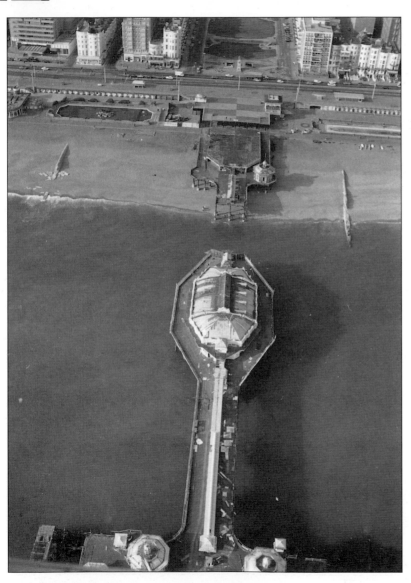

AERIAL VIEW OF THE WEST PIER

This aerial view of the West Pier, taken in the spring of 1988, shows the pier standing in three sections, following removal of the section described on the previous page. The new entrance deck, at the top of the picture, seems a very small part of the restoration compared to what obviously remained to be done at this time.

In 1996, £1 million was awarded from National Lottery funds for emergency repairs. Two years later, a further £14 million was forthcoming, but this was only about half of the estimated amount required and funds from other sources would be needed.

Early in 1999, former WBO super-middleweight boxer, Chris Eubank, of Hove, moved in to front a consortium to raise the necessary extra funding.

DEMOLITON OF COX'S FACTORY
AND THE LEWES ROAD VIADUCT

Cox's pill factory and the last section of the Lewes Road viaduct, were demolished in March 1983.

The site of Lewes Road Station, seen on page 44, was over by the trees at the end of the viaduct.

J S Sainsbury, would build a new superstore on the site; this is seen under construction in December 1984. The main facade of the store was given arches as a reminder of the vanished railway viaduct, and the original clock from Cox's frontage was installed. The store opened in April 1985, creating 150 jobs.

OPENING OF ASDA AT HOLLINGBURY

The huge Asda store at Hollingbury opened in November 1987, creating 420 jobs. It was the first superstore to open on the outskirts of Brighton; the second was the Gateway at Brighton Marina, a few days later. Many others have since followed, such as at the Holmbush Centre at Shoreham, causing concern for the way out-of-town shopping has developed, taking people away from established areas. In the spring of 1999 Asda was taken over by the American group Wal Mart.

COMMUNITY CHARGE DEMONSTRATION

Into the 1990s now and a photograph showing stroppy Brighton! 'Stuff The Poll Tax' reads a banner on the left. This rally was held on The Level in April 1990, to protest against the Community Charge – or poll tax as it came to be called – brought in by the goverment to replace the rating system.

Many of those at the rally burnt the bills they had received, intending not to pay the charge.

The view looks east, towards the Technical College, prominent in the background. The lack of trees on The Level is the after-effect of the great storm of October 1987.

BRIGHTON BEGGARS

A beggar asks for money – and gets it – at the top of Duke Street, in August 1991. West Street forms the background.

Begging had become commonplace in certain streets of Brighton by the 1990s, and was seen as extremely detrimental to the town by residents, the local authority, business people and visitors. Many beggars sat on shop steps and declared their reduced circumstances on cardboard notices, claiming that they were homeless, jobless, or both. Some were extremely aggressive in their demands for money from passers-by.

But this situation was nothing new for Brighton. The streets of Georgian and Victorian Brighton were very similar, although few beggars then could write!

Homelessness had been a concern in Brighton from the 1920s onwards. In 1999 it was estimated that some forty people were sleeping rough on Brighton's streets each night.

BUILDING THE OAK HOTEL

After nearly twenty-five years, a building finally went up on the site of the SS Brighton. The Oak Hotel is seen here under construction, first in May 1990, then again, below, nearing completion in April 1991. It would open with 138 bedrooms six months later. An Odeon cinema alongside was demolished at the same time and rebuilt as offices. The name chosen for this hotel was

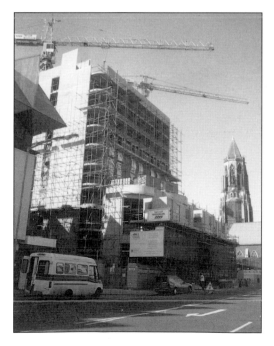

particularly apt as, in the 1600s, the site was occupied by an inn known as the George. This is where Charles II arrived in October 1651, having lost the battle of Worcester in the Civil War, to meet boat-owner Nicholas Tettersall. He took Charles in his brig, *The Surprise*, from Shoreham to France and temporary exile. At some time during his flight to Sussex, the King is supposed to have hidden in an oak tree to elude capture, so whoever decided to give the new hotel the name Oak had clearly done his or her homework. Unfortunately for local history, it was renamed the Quality Hotel early in 1999.

TRAM DEMONSTRATION

Traffic build-up and congestion in Brighton was another huge concern of the post-war period, particularly with the rise of environmental issues and fears that global warming was being accelerated by car exhaust fumes.

One spin-off from this was that trams made a short comeback to Brighton. For a week in July 1994, a 'People Mover' tram was demonstrated in New Road to coincide with an environmental conference in the town. It was operated by Parry People Movers of the West Midlands. The company stressed the 'green' advantages of such a system in its brochure, calling it 'the green machine'.

'Trams are the greenest form of transport after the bicycle and in a lightweight form are the ideal system for moving people about small town centres,' said the brochure.

While it generated a lot of interest as a fun novelty ride, nothing came of it and, as the century turns, some areas of central Brighton grind towards total gridlock, where traffic can't move for substantial periods of time.

FASHION SHOW

This group of young people, wearing a startling array of erotic jewellery – and not much else – paraded on the seafront in the summer of 1998, after being thrown off the Palace Pier for being too provocative.

They were publicising jewellery for sale at a shop in the North Laine area, with an impromptu fashion show.

Nearly all of them had body piercing of one sort of another – the latest fashion craze – including studs through their tongues. A few people were genuinely offended, many wanted a second look, but others just glanced, gave half a shrug, half a sigh, as if to say 'Well, this is Brighton!'

BRIGHTON PRIDE PARADE

Brighton has always welcomed those with an individual outlook on life and the town now hosts a large gay and lesbian community.

These photographs of August 1998

show their Brighton Pride carnival procession making its way along the seafront to Preston Park, via London Road – the main event in a week of partying, clubbing and beauty queen contests.

LAST ALBION MATCH
AT THE GOLDSTONE GROUND

Fans of Brighton and Hove Albion will instantly recognise the photographs here – the team's last match at the Goldstone Ground, Hove, after a residency of ninety-four years. The match was in April 1997, against Doncaster Rovers, with the Albion winning 1–0.

At the end of the game, fans dug up the pitch, pulled down the posts and ripped seats from the stands, partly to get mementos, but also to express anger at the way the ground had been sold off to pay massive £6 million debts – before any new stadium was in place.

The team spent the next two seasons in exile, playing at Gillingham, a round trip for fans of 160

miles. A new board decided on Withdean Stadium as a temporary home. Despite opposition from residents, Brighton and Hove Council granted permission in June 1998, for the Albion to play at Withdean for three years. There was no match at the stadium, due to legal delays, until July 1999, when a friendly against Nottingham Forest was played.

The club wanted a new 15,000 seat stadium at Falmer. In May 1999, a town poll supported this move. When the planning application is made, a public enquiry into the viability of the proposal will almost certainly be ordered.

FIRE AT THE ROYAL ALBION HOTEL

November 1998; a large section of the historic Royal Albion Hotel, opposite the Palace Pier, goes up in flames. Breakfast sausages caught fire in the kitchen and the flames shot straight up an extraction unit to the roof. Sixteen fire tenders and at least 160 fireman fought the blaze, using water pumped from the sea. Some 150 guests were evacuated, although one couple, in room 153, slept soundly through several hours of the drama. The repair bill was estimated at £7 million.

The Royal Albion opened in 1826 (as just the Albion), on a site previously occupied by a large mansion known as Russell House. This was built in 1755 for Dr Richard Russell, the Lewes physician mentioned in the introduction, who pioneered the sea-water cure for glandular disorders, bringing the first fashionable visitors to the town.

NEW YEAR'S EVE CROWDS

Pleasure-seeking crowds began this look at Brighton, and they end it. It is New Year's Eve 1998, and 10,000 people pack the Steine to welcome in the penultimate year of the century. With bands providing live music and fireworks at midnight, this was seen as a rehearsal for New Year's Eve 1999, when the century would finally turn (some would argue that that wouldn't really happen until the end of the year 2000). Although the celebrations went well, bottle fights were witnessed, pubs charged extortionate prices for rounds of drinks and the police cells ended up packed with drunks.

Photograph: Ray Ede

ABOUT THE AUTHOR

Chris Horlock was born, brought up and educated in Brighton. His father worked for the Kemp Town Brewery. At present he lives at Shoreham and teaches at Thomas a Becket Middle School, Worthing, where he is Head of Year 7.

He has a finger in many extra-curricular pies, including graphic art, musical theatre and local history. The first photographs in his Brighton collection were taken in the summer of 1968. His brother had bought a 'proper' camera and on the initial try-out went around Brighton taking views of Churchill Square under construction, the Hippodrome newly converted to a bingo hall and the then recently-built Brighton Square.

In the 1970s several books came out showing views of old Brighton. These fired up Chris's interest on how the town looked in the past and started him collecting old views of Brighton in earnest.

For nearly twenty years he was a regular visitor to the home of James Gray (1904-1998), historian and author, discussing every aspect of the town's development and studying his extensive annotated collection of Brighton and Hove photographs.

Today, Chris lectures (and now writes) on aspects of the town's history and his own collection of Brighton photographs is approaching 6,000 – and still growing. His next book, *Brighton, The Century in Photographs, Volume II*, will be published at the end of 2000 and he has plans for two more Brighton books in 2001.